WORKING IN PARTNERSHIP

Working in Partnership

Best practice in customer–supplier relations

Bernard Burnes and Barrie Dale

Gower

Published by
Gower Publishing Limited
Gower House
Croft Road
Aldershot
Hampshire GU11 3HR
England

Gower
Old Post Road
Brookfield
Vermont 05036
USA

Bernard Burnes and Barrie Dale have asserted their right under the Copyright, Designs and Patents Act 1988 to be identified as the authors of this work.

British Library Cataloguing in Publication Data
Burnes, Bernard:
   Working in partnership : best practice in customer–supplier relations
   1. Industrial procurement 2. Relationship marketing
   3. Customer relations
   I. Title II. Dale, Barrie G, 1947
   658.7

ISBN 0 566 07997 6

Dale. B. G.
   Working in partnership : best practice in customer-supplier relations / Bernard Burnes and Barrie Dale
       p.   cm.
   Includes index.
   ISBN 0-566-07997-6 (hc)
   1. Industrial procurement. 2. Negotiation in business.
I. Burnes, Bernard. 1953-   . II. Title.
HD39.5.D35   1998   - 97-42340
658.8—dc21   CIP

Typeset in Palatino 11/13pt by Saxon Graphics Ltd., Derby and printed in Great Britain by M P G Books Limited, Bodmin

Contents

List of figures   ix
List of contributors   xi
Preface   xv
Glossary of terms   xvii

Introduction   1
Bernard Burnes and Barrie Dale
Long-term business partnerships   2
Barriers to developing partnerships   4
Organization of the book   7

1 The Implications and Reality of Partnership   9
   Steve New
   The research   10
   Results   11
   The reality of partnership   12
   The persistence of power   17
   Some lessons   18

2   **Competitive Tendering and Partnership in
    the Public Sector**   21
    Andrew Erridge
    Analysing competition   21
    Constraints on the application of partnership   22
    Legislation and policy on public procurement   24
    Financial accountability   25
    Competitive tendering for services   27
    Internal market for healthcare and social services   30
    Economic and social policy objectives   33
    How different is the public sector?   34
    Conclusion   35

3   **The Automotive Industry – the Customer's Perspective:
    a Study of the Rover Group**   39
    Garry B Grove
    Strategic influences in the delivery of change within
       partnership relations at Rover – 'The Rover Way'   40
    Purchasing quality strategy   42
    Best practice   46
    'Rover Tomorrow' strategy   47
    Closing the competitive gap   49
    Distribution efficiency   50
    Relationship transformation – building bridges and
       developing trust   52
    Benefits, obstacles and progress   53
    The way forward – Rover and its suppliers   55

4   **The Automotive Industry – the Supplier's Perspective:
    a Study of Tallent Engineering**   59
    Clive Wheeler
    Pressures for change   60
    Conflict versus co-operation   60
    Working with customers   63
    Taking the initiative with customers   65
    Changing attitudes, structures and practices   67
    Going down the supply chain   69
    Benefits and lessons learnt   70
    Footnote: July 1997   72

5 **Supplier Partnerships: a Study of Cosalt Holiday Homes**   **75**
    Mike J. Isaac
    Cosalt's quality programme   75
    The rationale behind supplier partnership   77
    The grounding of a supplier partnership strategy   77
    Methodology for small- and medium-size enterprises
       (SMEs)   78
    Strategic supplier partnership versus short-term   81
    Findings, achievements and failures   85
    Summary   88

6 **Supplier Partnerships: Assessing the Potential and
    Getting Started**   **91**
    Bernard Burnes and Paul Whittle
    What is supplier partnership?   92
    Step 1: Should you consider supplier partnership?   93
    Step 2: Benefits and drawbacks   94
    Step 3: Developing an action plan   95
    Step 4: Getting started   97
    Summary   99

7 **Developing the Partnership Concept for the Future**   **101**
    Bernard Burnes and Steve New
    Identifying the basics   103
    Three approaches to partnership   104
    Selecting an approach and measuring the benefits   107
    The supply chain improvement process   108

8 **Customer–Supplier Relations – Tools, Techniques and
    Systems**   **111**
    Barrie Dale and Bernard Burnes
    Getting started   112
    Developing the benefits   118
    Monitoring the relationship   142
    Conclusions   145

9 **Developing Partnerships: Epilogue**   **149**
    Bernard Burnes and Barrie Dale

Putting your own house in order   151
The process of partnership   155
Potential difficulties of partnerships   158
Conclusions   159

Index   163

Figures

1.1 Partnership relations with customers   12
1.2 Partnership relations with suppliers   13
1.3 Customers' partnership behaviour   15
1.4 Suppliers' partnership behaviour   16
3.1 Relationship between quality strategy and purchasing quality strategy   43
3.2 'Rover Tomorrow' strategy   48
3.3 A strategic transformation   52
3.4 Supplier development process vision   53
4.1 Conflict to co-operation: summary of trends   61
4.2 The cost squeeze   74
5.1 Flow diagram for SMEs embarking upon supplier development   79
5.2 Supplier development meeting agenda   82
5.3 Checklist for evaluating supplier development performance   84
7.1 The three approaches to partnership – pros and cons   106
8.1 Cause and effect diagram   120
8.2 Corrugator design of experiments and test results   125
8.3 Failure mode and effects analysis   128

8.4   Flow chart for Ferranti PECs – core failures   131
8.5   L-type matrix diagram for customer loyalty
         programme   134
8.6   Quality function deployment analysis   138
8.7   Statistical process control chart   143

List of contributors

Bernard Burnes joined the Manchester School of Management in 1985. He holds a degree in Economic and Social History and a PhD in Organizational Psychology. He originally trained and worked as a design engineer. Dr Burnes' main research and teaching interests revolve around strategy, organizational change and supply chain management.

Dr Burnes has worked with a wide range of private and public sector organizations, including the National Economic Development Council, Nissan Motor Manufacturing (UK) Ltd and Rover Group Ltd. He has authored 4 books and over 60 academic articles and book chapters. He is also Director of the UMIST Supplier Development Centre and also Joint Editor of the *International Journal of Operations and Production Management*.

Barrie Dale is the United Utilities Professor of Quality Management. He has been researching quality management since 1981, receiving research grants of over £3 million, and has written 7 books and over 290 papers on the subject. He is an academician of the International Academy for Quality, co-editor of the *International Journal of Quality and Reliability Management* and Editor of the McGraw Hill 'Quality in Action' series. He has been closely involved in the Hong Kong Government 'Make it Better in Hong Kong' Campaign and is international quality management advisor to the South African Quality Institute. He is also a Director of the Trafford Park Business Forum.

Andrew Erridge is Senior Lecturer in the School of Public Policy, Economics and Law at the University of Ulster. He is responsible for postgraduate courses and research in Strategic Procurement Management. His main research interest is in public procurement. Amongst his publications is a book entitled *Managing Purchasing: Sourcing and Contracting* and articles in journals including *Public Money and Management, Management Education and Development* and the *European Journal of Purchasing and Supply Management*, of which he is a member of the Editorial Committee. He was a founder member and former chair of the International Purchasing and Supply Education and Research Association.

Garry Grove is a Director of Purchasing, Rover Group. He joined Standard Triumph Coventry, Car Division of British Leyland Motor Corporation as a Commercial Apprentice and in 1975 he became Production Materials Buyer for Jaguar Rover Triumph Specialist Cars Division. In 1982 he joined Land Rover Vehicles at Solihull as Chief Buyer-Production Materials, responsible for electrical/electronics, body hardware, power train and trim commodities at various stages. In 1989 he became Purchase Timing Manager responsible for all Land Rover's 4 × 4 product programmes. Subsequently he became Purchase Director – Facilities and General Services, responsible for all capital plant facilities, infrastructure contracts, including energy, systems, consumables for all Rover sites and Business Unit Operations. He is now Production Purchasing Director – Power Train and Chassis, responsible for a total of £1.60 bn spend (with c. 280 suppliers) based at Longbridge. He is also Strategy Champion (Ownership) within Purchasing's Quality Strategy.

Dr Mike Isaac held the position of Joint Managing Director of Cosalt Holiday Homes Limited in Hull until August 1997. He is currently Managing Director of ABI Caravans in Beverley. He worked for BSC Llanwern for 12 years followed by 3 years as a Manufacturing Manager with Halmanco, the cycle manufacturers. Further managerial positions were held in the construction industry prior to joining Cosalt in 1986, as Works Manager. In 1988 he was awarded an MBA degree followed by a PhD in 1995. He is also a professionally qualified Metallurgist. He has published several articles on supplier development and quality circles and is a visiting lecturer at UMIST.

Dr Steve New is a Fellow in Management Studies at Hertford College and University Lecturer in Operations Management. Formerly he was a lecturer at the Manchester School of Management, UMIST. His background includes a first degree in Physics, training as an engineering physicist with Rolls-Royce plc and a spell with management consultants Collinson Grant. His PhD research was undertaken at Manchester Business School, working with the Truck Components Division of Eaton Ltd. He has acted as a consultant for a number of organizations, including BICC, British Steel and GPT. His current research focuses on inter-organizational collaboration, supply chain management and the environmental performance of organizations.

Clive Wheeler is Operations Director, Tallent Engineering. After completing a BSc in Mechanical Engineering at City University, he began his working career at Thorn Lighting Ltd. In his sixteen years with Thorn, he held a number of posts including Production Superintendent, Production Manager, Personnel Manager and, from July 1987, Manufacturing Director of the Systems Lighting Division. In this time he also attended courses at Cranfield University and INSEAD, and made a one-month study visit to Japan. Since 1990, he has been in his present job where he has been involved in raising turnover from £28m to £60m and increasing quality from 2000 PPM to 25 PPM. Clive is also a Chartered Engineer, Member of the Institution of Electrical Engineers, and Founder Director of the Durham Training and Enterprise Council.

Paul Whittle is Operations Management Project Officer at UMIST. After graduating in 1984 in Physics, he worked for the GEC Hirst Research Centre on the development of processes and technologies for the manufacture of microelectronic devices. He then spent 2 years working on the design of a heat treatment cell for aluminium components as part of a Sheet Metal Flexible Manufacturing System for BAe. Subsequently he worked for AMTRI as a Manufacturing Systems Consultant on projects ranging from a CIM implementation to testing of designs for newsprint reel delivery systems. During his time at UMIST he has worked on Teaching Company programmes, Engineering Doctorate and (developed and delivered) strategy development workshops and continuous improvement training – mainly in the automotive component supply industry – as part of the Supplier Development Centre.

Preface

For the last three decades or so, a key feature of Japanese-based manufacturing companies has been their strong and close ties with their supplier communities. The benefits of such relationships are well documented and include joint problem solving leading to cost savings for customer and supplier alike; the expertise and technology which a supplier contributes to the development of the customer's design; joint long-term planning; improved knowledge of the systems, practices, processes, procedures and people of both parties; and sharing of information and facilities.

In more recent times such collaboration has started to happen in Europe, particularly in the automotive, electronics and consumer goods industries. Whilst some progress has been made, all has not gone smoothly due to the fear and mistrust which has been built up over the years. Some industries have only just started to realize the potential benefits of partnerships and others are still operating in an adversarial mode. There seems little doubt, however, that the trend towards building partnerships between customer and supplier will grow in importance in the future.

The main focus of this book is to provide guidance to organizations wishing to establish and develop partnerships with their customers and/or suppliers. It draws upon recent research and best practice from a variety of business environments. There are a number of textbooks which focus on quality management, purchasing and tools and techniques, but few which deal with the issue of partnership from an holistic standpoint. We hope that in this context the book will make a contribution to knowledge.

The book is targeted at those senior and middle management, and quality, purchasing and technical professionals who have responsibility in their organization for developing partnerships with their respective customers and/or suppliers. We believe that management at all levels of the organizational hierarchy will find something of value.

It is unlikely that the book will become the textbook of any undergraduate or postgraduate course offered in Europe at universities and business schools since, as far as we know, there are no partnership and supplier development options in existing course curriculums. This may change as more universities and business schools offer purchasing options in their courses. However, MBA students and postgraduates studying the subject of partnerships in TQM, purchasing, logistics, operations management and marketing options will find the book of value, as will those studying for professional examinations or undergoing post-experience training which involves these aspects. The growing band of academics teaching and researching aspects relating to partnerships and supplier development should also find the book helpful.

As editors, we have made a conscious effort to keep the text free from jargon. We should also add that apart from the chapters bearing one of or both our names, the views and opinions expressed by individual contributors are their own. In compiling the text, we have not set out to produce a weighty tome, but rather to distil, in summary form, the key learning lessons in partnerships. We believe this aim has been met and sincerely hope you, the reader, concur with this view. Any ideas for improvement, however, will be warmly received.

Finally, we wish to thank all the contributors for making this book possible. We have learned much from them. We hope our readers will too.

B. Burnes and B.G. Dale,
Manchester School of Management,
UMIST

Glossary of terms

AQP	Advanced quality planning
ASQC	American Society for Quality Control
BEMs	Business effectiveness measures
BPR	Business process re-engineering
CBI	Confederation of British Industry
CCT	Compulsory competitive tendering
CEO	Chief executive officer
CMI	Co-managed inventory
CSF	Critical success factors
CUP	Central Unit on Procurement
DHSS	Department of Health and Social Security
DMUs	Direct managed units
DPA	Departmental purpose analysis
DSOs	Direct service organizations
DTI	Department of Trade and Industry
EC	European Community

ECM	Effective cost management
EDI	Electronic data interchange
FMEA	Failure mode and effects analysis
GM	General Motors
GPFHs	General practitioner fund holders
HMSO	Her Majesty's Stationery Office
IIP	Investors in people
IOL	Institute of Logistics
IT	Information technology
JIT	Just in time
MD	Managing director
MOD	Ministry of Defence
MRP	Materials requirements planning
NEDO	National Economic Development Office
NHS	National Health Service
NMUK	Nissan Motor Manufacturing (UK) Ltd
NPI	New product introduction
NX95	Nissan Excellence in 1995
OEM	Original equipment manufacturers
PAC	Public accounts committee
PDSA	Plan, do, study, act
PMP	Project management process
PPM	Parts per million
QAF	Quotation analysis form
QCCs	Quality control circles
QCD	Quality, cost, delivery
QCDDM	Quality, cost, delivery, development and management
QFD	Quality function deployment
QOS	Quality operating system

REAL	Rover employee assisted learning
RLB	Rover Learning Business
RPN	Risk priority number
SCG	Strategy core group
SDT	Supplier development teams
SMEs	Small and medium-sized enterprises
SMED	Single minute exchange of die
SMMT	Society of Motor Manufacturers and Traders
SPC	Statistical process control
SQA	Supplier quality assurance
SQI	Supplier quality improvement
SWOT	Strengths, weaknesses, opportunities and threats
TBP	Total business performance
TEL	Tallent Engineering Ltd
TPM	Total productive maintenance
TQI	Total quality improvement
TQM	Total quality management
TX95	Tallent Excellence in 1995
UK	United Kingdom
UMIST	University of Manchester Institute of Science and Technology
VFM	Value for money
VMI	Vendor managed inventory

Introduction

Bernard Burnes and Barrie Dale

The quality of purchased supplies is crucial to a purchasing organization's products and services and consequently to its success in the market place. Bought-in components and services may often account for some 70 to 80 per cent of the final manufacturing costs so it is clear that suppliers are critical to the cost base of the purchaser. Many leading European companies, following the example of Japan, have during the last decade or so started to encourage their suppliers to develop their quality management systems, adopt a continuous improvement philosophy, eliminate non-value added activity, improve their manufacturing systems, become more flexible and responsive, and reduce costs.

This process of the customers working together with their suppliers to effect these changes is given a variety of names, such as supplier development, co-makership, partnership sourcing, customer–supplier alliances, and pro-active purchasing. This variety of names, and the way different organizations interpret them and the process, has led to much confusion about both the meaning and practicality of the partnership approach to purchasing. The purpose of this book is to examine both the theory and practice of partnerships and show how the approach can be applied and bring benefits to organizations in a range of industries.

This chapter begins by examining the case for customer–supplier partnerships and the typical obstacles. It then goes on to describe the remainder of the book.

Long-term business partnerships

The traditional and open-market bargaining approach to customer–supplier dealings is based on the assumption that they are adversaries with differing objectives, engaged in a win–lose contest represented by tough negotiations and cost undercutting. This approach focuses on negative issues and is characterized by uncertainty which has led to the destruction of businesses.

Partnership demands a new form of relationship. It means working together towards a common goal, based on the principle that both parties can gain more benefit through co-operation than by separately pursuing their own self-interests. It means establishing a relationship based on common aims and aspirations, mutual trust and commitment, integrity, integration, co-operation, honesty, open declaration of problems, a willingness to work together to find answers to problems, sharing of data and ideas, improvements and best practices, clearly understood responsibilities, collaborative research and development work and a desire to continuously improve the product and service. This form of relationship has similarities with a vertically integrated firm but without the difficulties of managing a complex business across different types of technologies and processes.

To develop a viable long-term business relationship, considerable changes in behaviour and attitude are required in both the customer and supplier organizations which need to be fostered. Customers must be prepared to develop plans and procedures for working with suppliers and commit resources to this. On the other hand, suppliers have to accept full responsibility for the quality of their shipped product and not rely on the customer's receiving inspection. As a prerequisite of partnership, both parties have to reach an agreement on how they will work together, what they want from the relationship and how to resolve any problems which may arise. To ensure that the relationship is sustainable it is important that the objectives of the agreement should be analysed and discussed on a regular basis.

The typical benefits of working in partnerships include:

- Reduction and elimination of the inspection of supplied parts and materials.
- Improved product and service quality, delivery performance and responsiveness.
- Improved productivity, lower inventory carrying costs and reduced costs per piece.
- Value for money purchases.
- Security and stability of supplies.
- Transfer of ideas and expertise between customer and supplier and dissemination of best practice.
- Joint problem-solving activities, with the customer providing assistance to the supplier to help improve processes, leading to easier and faster resolution of problems.
- Integration of business practices and procedures between customer and supplier.
- A comprehensive customer–supplier communications network to ensure the supplier is provided with early access to customer future designs and manufacturing plans and is kept informed of changing customer requirements. This assists with the planning of workloads and would typically open up wider channels than those in the traditional relationship where the buyer and sales representatives would be the main point of contact.
- Customer and supplier are more willing and open to examine their processes to look for improvements.
- The supplier contributes to the customer's design process, undertakes development work and monitors technological trends; this can lead to new innovative products.
- Helping to develop sustainable growth of the supplier in terms of investment in equipment and manufacturing resources. Related to this is the reputation and credibility in the market place which arises from the relationship.

- Exposure of the supplier to new tools, techniques, systems and business practices.
- Provision by the customer of an advisory service to suppliers in terms of training, equipment and operating methods.

Barriers to developing partnerships

Developing partnerships is not without difficulties. Lascelles and Dale (1990) have carried out research which reveals that the following aspects of the customer–supplier relationship can act as a barrier to supplier development:

- poor communication and feedback
- supplier complacency
- misguided supplier improvement objectives
- lack of customer credibility as viewed by their suppliers, and
- misconceptions regarding purchasing power.

Poor communication and feedback
In general, communication and feedback between customer and supplier is not good. Indeed, both parties sometimes do not realize how poor they are at communicating with each other. The main dissatisfactions expressed by suppliers relates to technical specifications and requirements, the lack of consultation on design and product engineering aspects and changes to the delivery schedule. There are strong indications that not all dissatisfied suppliers actually communicate their dissatisfaction to the customer.

Supplier complacency
Suppliers are often unconcerned about customer satisfaction. There are two types of measurement relating to a customer's satisfaction with the quality of supplies: reactive and proactive. Examples of reactive measures include:

- failure data (e.g. non-conformity analysis, customer rejections, warranty claims)
- customer assessment rating and audit reports

- verbal feedback from meetings with customers
- contractual requirements outlined in the customers' vendor improvement plans.

Examples of proactive measures include:

- customer workshops and forum meetings
- market research
- benchmarking key processes
- evaluating competitors' products
- reliability analysis
- advanced quality planning carried out in conjunction with customers.

Misguided supplier improvement objectives

Customers are often not sure what they want from supplier improvement initiatives and can underestimate the time and resources required to introduce and develop partnerships. There also appears to be a dilution and distortion of the quality message as requirements are passed down the supply chain. For example, when faced with demands to improve quality from customers, suppliers usually react by implementing specific tools and techniques, and in turn insist that their own suppliers use the same. They fail to understand that these reactions are only fully effective within the context of an organization-wide approach to continuous improvement.

Lack of customer credibility

Suppliers need to be convinced that a customer is serious about continuous improvement. The customer's behaviour and attitudes must be consistent with what they are saying to suppliers. The following examples show how a credibility gap may emerge.

- Purchasing and supplies management practices, such as a competitive pricing policy, frequent switches from one supplier to another, unpredictable and inflated production schedules, last-minute changes to schedules, poor engineering design/production/supplier liaison, inconsistent decisions made by supplier quality assurance (SQA) personnel, over-stringent specifications, abuse of power by SQA personnel and the use of 'loss of business' as a bargaining ploy in negotiating a reduction in price. It is not uncommon for a customer to talk quality to its suppliers and then act quite differently by relegating quality to secondary importance behind, for example, price and meeting the production schedule.

- The TQM and business excellence image which leading purchasing organizations attempt to create in discussions with suppliers are not reflected in reality when supplier personnel visit their own manufacturing sites.
- A customer accepts non-conforming items over a long period of time, even if unwittingly, and then criticizes the supplier for supplying non-conforming materials.
- A lack of strategy for dealing with the tooling used for supplied parts. For example, a supplier reports to the customer that the customer-supplied tooling is reaching the end of its useful life. The customer then asks the supplier to carry out some minor refurbishment as a short-term measure. The supplier advises against this strategy, but is pressurized to do the repairs. When non-conforming parts are found in batches from the 'patched-up' tooling, the supplier acquires from the customer quality performance demerits.
- The customer fails to respond to a supplier's request for information and to provide advice on queries.
- The supplier uses components which have not passed the initial sample approval procedure.
- The customer's SQA personnel are fooled by the camouflage measures, fakes and ruses employed by a supplier in an assessment of their quality system.
- The supplier is forced to hold stocks to cover the customer's inadequate scheduling and poor systems control.

Purchasing power: a misconception

Purchasing power is a critical issue in the buyer–supplier relationship. Lack of purchasing power is a commonly cited reason for the lack of success in improving supplier performance. The general view is that a purchaser's influence on its suppliers varies with its purchasing power, and the greater the power the more effective will be its SQA activities. These power imbalances can cause uneven levels of commitment in the relationship.

Purchasing power alone is no guarantee of improving supplier performance. Companies with considerable purchasing power may well improve the quality of purchased items, but will not necessarily achieve lasting benefits or motivate their suppliers to internalize the benefits of a process of continuous improvement to satisfy all their customers.

Having described some of the benefits of, and barriers to, partnerships we can now proceed to describe the remainder of this book.

Organization of the book

The nine chapters which follow are designed to flesh out the concept and practice of customer–supplier partnerships. Chapter 1 presents recent research carried out by Steve New of Hertford College, Oxford. The research shows that not all companies are ready for, or can achieve, partnerships with their customers and suppliers. However, if they recognize their own circumstances and develop an appropriate strategy, they should be able to establish effective collaborations with their customers/suppliers. Chapter 2, by Andrew Erridge of the University of Ulster, describes the approach to partnerships which is emerging in the public sector. He argues that whilst developments such as competitive tendering may seem to prevent partnerships, in reality such developments are both possible and beneficial.

Chapters 3 to 5 are by practising managers who describe the approach and benefits of partnerships in their companies and their industries. Chapter 3 is by Garry Grove who is a Director of Purchasing in the Rover Group. He describes the development of purchasing at Rover, its approach to supplier partnerships and the benefits it brings. Chapter 4, by Clive Wheeler who is Operations Director at Tallent Engineering, covers the supplier's perspective. It describes how Tallent has built a reputation as a leading supplier of automotive parts over the past 15 years and shows how it is possible for a supplier to work co-operatively with a variety of customers each of whom have their own distinct approach and definition of partnership. Chapter 5, by Mike Isaac, who was until recently Managing Director of Cosalt Holiday Homes, shows how a medium-sized enterprise involved in assembling caravans has developed partnerships, often with much larger suppliers.

Chapters 6 to 8 provide practical advice on developing and maintaining partnerships. Chapter 6, by Burnes and Whittle, provides straightforward and practical guidelines for starting and maintaining a supplier development programme. Chapter 7, by Burnes and New, shows the need for organizations to identify what type of partnership to establish with their suppliers and what tools and techniques are effective in each. In Chapter 8, Dale and Burnes examine the tools and techniques that companies can use in developing and maintaining partnerships. A number of the contributors have mentioned the tools and techniques they use and we believe it is helpful to the readers to include a stand-alone chapter which provides a brief summary of them together with an outline of the ISO 9000 series of quality management systems.

The concluding chapter summarizes the key lessons that can be learnt from the contributors in terms of starting and developing customer–supplier partnerships, the requirements for successful partnerships and the potential difficulties which need to be overcome.

Further reading

Lascelles D.M., and Dale, B.G. (1990), 'Examining the barriers to supplier development,' *International Journal of Quality and Reliability Management*, 7 (2), pp. 46–56.

1 The implications and reality of partnership

Steve New

The notion of partnership in buyer–seller relations reflects the convergence of several streams of management thought. From an operations perspective, the emergence of TQM has been a main source of inspiration, as has the development of the concept of the supply chain in logistics. In parallel, marketing experts have come to a clearer appreciation of the importance of stable relationships between buying and selling firms and of interorganizational networks.

For those trying to grapple with what partnership means for their organization, the array of different approaches and terminology can seem perplexing. Furthermore, the examples used as evidence for the partnership ideal are often drawn from only a few industries who were early exponents of the concept, i.e. the automotive and electronics industries, and many managers complain that the translation to their situation is less than straightforward. Part of the problem is that whilst partnership is such an attractive and simple concept, it is not easy to put into practice.

This chapter looks at some of the practical implications of partnership for buyers and suppliers, and explores how firms can develop effective and sustainable co-operation. Its purpose is to show that there are many options for structuring partnership relationships, and that it is possible to obtain benefits progressively rather than adopt partnership as a whole package. Furthermore, effective collaboration is often possible even if there are imbalances of power between the buyer and supplier. The chapter opens with a description of a research project conducted by the author and management consultants A.T. Kearney in conjunction with the UK Institute of Logistics (IOL), followed by a discussion of the main findings and the implications for partnerships.

The research

The research was unusual both in that it combined two sources of data and it was the result of co-operation between academics and consultants. The first source of data was a six-page questionnaire which was mailed in early 1994 to the membership of the UK Institute of Logistics with the magazine *Logistics Focus*. This was complemented by seven panel meetings at which senior managers from a range of industries were invited to discuss their experiences. These meetings were based around dinner parties in which the after-dinner discussion was tape-recorded and video-taped. Each event contained a brief presentation designed to stimulate controversy and discussion.

The panel meetings were informal and the participants were relatively unaffected by the presence of the audio and video recorders. A total of 51 managers were involved, in meetings which ranged in size from three to thirteen participants (plus two to three researchers from UMIST and A.T. Kearney). Two of the meetings only involved firms in the automotive sector, and another concentrated mainly on retailing and consumer goods. The remainder were mixed, and included, for example, managers from a greetings card manufacturer comparing experiences with a pharmaceutical multinational and a small firm making industrial springs. The invitees were drawn from two main sources: personal contacts of A.T. Kearney and UMIST who were known to be active or interested in supply chain management issues, and early respondents to the questionnaire who had expressed an interest in participation. A smaller number were people who had read about the launch of the project in the trade press and had made direct contact with the author.

The questionnaire was designed jointly by A.T. Kearney and UMIST. Approximately 11,000 copies were distributed, with 273 usable copies returned. This low response rate (2.5 per cent) may be explained by the length of the questionnaire and also the fact that there were nineteen other separate pieces of literature included with that issue of the magazine. Normally the danger of low response rates is that they introduce a self-selection bias in the respondents, but in this case the mailing did not go to a neutral cross-section of managers or firms; the membership of IOL is already biased to those individuals with an interest in supply chain issues, and those firms in which the activity has some profile. The 'sample' of both elements in the work reflects a population of interested and perhaps curious managers who have some sort of pre-commitment to the idea of supply chain integration. The quantitative analysis of this work, while suggesting trends and connections, cannot be used as a definitive description of UK managers' views. Nevertheless the responses did reflect a broad range of respondent organizations, in terms of size of firm and industrial sector.

Results

Partnerships are popular. Both the survey and panel components of the research confirmed that the participating organizations were facing considerable competitive pressures. There was a strong emphasis on improving customer satisfaction. In particular, respondents generally reported significant improvements in customer service combined with reductions in lead times and all forms of inventory, particularly raw materials. Many participants in the panel meeting confirmed that achieving target improvements necessitated close co-operation with suppliers and corporate customers.

The results of the survey suggest that the concept of partnership was popular. Figures 1.1 and 1.2 show the status of partner-

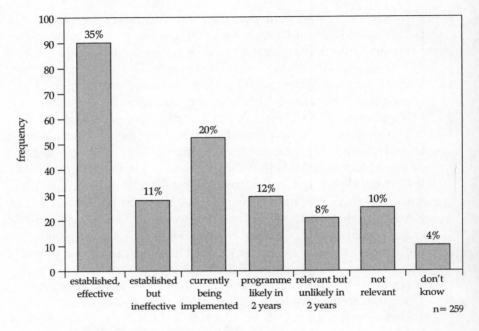

Figure 1.1   Partnership relations with customers

ships within the organizations, and indicate that the majority had, or were pursuing, partnerships in both directions. Those who claimed that such partnerships were not relevant included those who had no corporate customers (such as retailers) and those who had no direct suppliers associated with the supply chain (such as third-party transport firms). The acceptance of the idea of partnerships, therefore, is widespread amongst the participating firms. This reinforced the view that the notion of partnership has achieved the status of orthodoxy amongst those concerned with supply chain management.

The reality of partnership

The research suggested, however, that there was widespread scepticism regarding the concept of partnership and that the

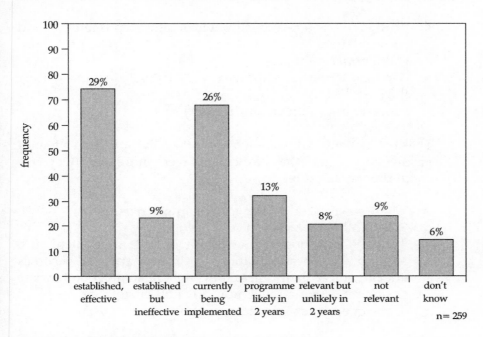

Figure 1.2   Partnership relations with suppliers

practice did not always match the ideals of the concept. The word partnership was subject to a multitude of interpretations, ranging from giving price discounts to customers who provided steady volumes of work (an industrial service company), to complex risk and revenue sharing partnerships for new product development (in high technology manufacturing). Despite the substance of these arrangements, participants were often keen to point out that partnership was not a soft or cosy option. Typical comments included:

- 'A partnership isn't always "hold hands and walk off into the sunset."'
  (Manufacturer)
- 'I don't like the word partnership for a start. I believe that it's a professional, meaningful business relationship.'
  (Manufacturer)

- 'Partnership is a relationship which allows co-operation and co-ordination.'
  (Automotive supplier)
- 'We look to partnerships as a way of stabilizing and getting the best deal ...'
  (Consumer product manufacturer)

These statements fall somewhat short of the idealized view of partnership. Some other participants were more overtly cynical about the whole concept:

- 'There's a lot of screwing goes on in partnerships.'
  (Chemical manufacturer)
- 'We're only making partnerships in order to try and enhance our own business situation ... if that partner becomes uncompetitive then unless they've built some good barriers to stop me moving I will move to another supplier.'
  (Consumer goods supplier)

These comments provide an interesting foil to the quantitative results of the survey: reported actions did not *necessarily* concur with managers' aspirations. Respondents were asked to score their agreement with a series of issues which focused on partnership-type behaviour between the respondent's firm and its customers and with its suppliers. The first set of statements relates to relationships with customers, and provides a picture of industrial practice that is somewhat removed from the partnership ideal. In particular, the sharing of detailed cost information scores low (see Figure 1.3), whilst there is considerable agreement that customers use threats to secure low prices.

The analysis is developed by examining the difference in responses between firms who claimed to have established effective partnerships with customers and those who did not. Whilst there are some statistically significant differences in the direction that one would expect, there is nevertheless considerable spread amongst the responses for the partnership group. The largest differences appear to relate to operational aspects of working together; there is only weak support for partnership

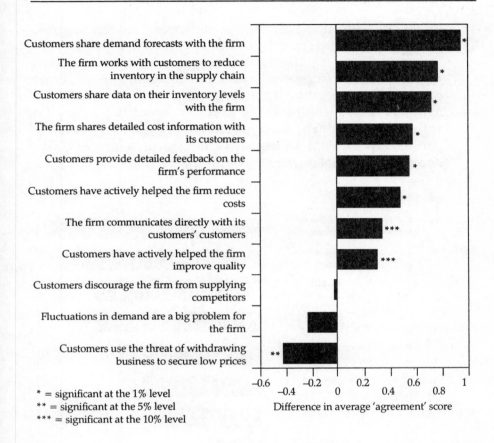

Customers share demand forecasts with the firm

The firm works with customers to reduce inventory in the supply chain

Customers share data on their inventory levels with the firm

The firm shares detailed cost information with its customers

Customers provide detailed feedback on the firm's performance

Customers have actively helped the firm reduce costs

The firm communicates directly with its customers' customers

Customers have actively helped the firm improve quality

Customers discourage the firm from supplying competitors

Fluctuations in demand are a big problem for the firm

Customers use the threat of withdrawing business to secure low prices

* = significant at the 1% level
** = significant at the 5% level
*** = significant at the 10% level

Difference in average 'agreement' score

Figure 1.3   Customers' partnership behaviour

firms sharing cost data or being less vulnerable to customer threats.

Contrasting these results with those for suppliers raises some interesting questions. Two features stand out: firstly, there is little evidence of the sharing of cost data. Secondly, respondents seem to consistently rate their own relationships with suppliers as more co-operative than their relationships with customers. As the respondents were drawn from a wide variety of firms at different stages of supply chains, this indicates a strange asymmetry of perception. Figure 1.4 indicates a similar pattern to that shown in Figure 1.3; the main differences associated with partnership relate to the operational issues of sharing demand forecasts and co-operating to reduce costs and inventory. The marginal difference in average scores in regard to the threat of withdrawing business is not statistically significant. Proclaimed partnership does not necessarily seem to mean a firm will abandon its commercial power.

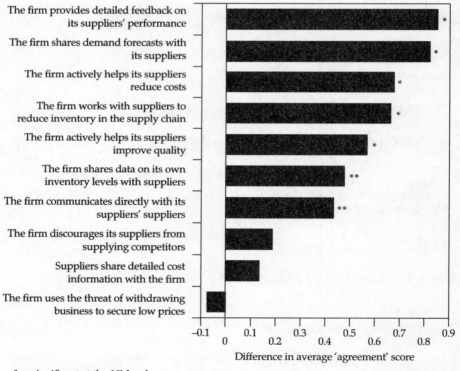

* = significant at the 1% level
** = significant at the 5% level
*** = significant at the 10% level

Figure 1.4   Suppliers' partnership behaviour

The persistence of power

The panel meetings were a rich source of insight into the importance of power in supply chain relationships. The following comments were typical:

- 'When power influences are brought into play then partnerships become an interesting concept, and not really supported by the reality of customer–supplier relationships.'
  (Automotive supplier)
- 'In the UK market we're in a situation where everyone believes it's dog eat dog out there; our culture is one where we don't believe in trust.'
  (Manufacturer)

Analysis of the survey responses suggests that the issue of power in supply chain relationships is important yet defies a simplistic analysis. From both the panel meetings and the questionnaire data, commercial power cannot be easily 'calculated' from a set of parameters. Whilst the number of competitors in a market, or relative size of firms, play a part, the relationship between firms seems to be governed to a significant extent by perceptions and emotions. A good example is provided by a comment from a manager of a large food multinational:

- 'If someone says do you want to be a partner to X (a major UK retailer), it is like saying does a minnow want to be eaten by a shark.'

Another manufacturer suggested that a large retailer (who happens to generate some publicity for its proclaimed partnership approach to suppliers) could ring up several times a day and threaten severe commercial sanctions (such as exclusion from television advertising arrangements) unless certain conditions were met instantly. Even amongst firms who wished to work collaboratively, there seemed little chance of abandoning the sanctions and mechanisms of the market.

Some lessons

Taken together, these findings suggest that whilst many firms are pursuing the goal of partnership, there may be more co-operation at the operational level – working together to make the system as a whole effective – than at the level of transforming the fundamentals of the commercial relationship. This conclusion was clearly reinforced by the panel discussions, where participants cited examples in which effective partnerships were formed at the operational level. For example, firms could work out systems for deliveries and packaging of mutual benefit to buyer and seller. However, these could be 'sabotaged' by interference from the sales and buying departments, who were manoeuvring to establish bargaining positions for the commercial negotiations:

- 'If we get logistics people in there, making a good "game plan", then suddenly sales and purchasing people hear about it and have another meeting ... and eventually the whole thing gets pulled down ... It's all about the actual power structures ... '
(Consumer goods manufacturer)

Nevertheless, some types of effective co-operation could be achieved as a 'conspiracy' by the logistic people against the purchasing and sales functions. Progress towards partnership at the operational level – in the spirit of improving the whole system – is sometimes possible in spite of a lack of trust or commitment at the commercial level.

A further lesson that emerged from the work is that whilst the question of power cannot be wished away (as perhaps is the case in some treatments of partnership) one of the most significant barriers to developing co-operation is the perceived potential for the abuse of power.

The issue of perception is of practical importance because it suggests that organizations should be wary of relying on caricatures or partial models of their customers' and their own demeanour towards suppliers. There is a danger of believing that your customers are worse than they are, and of believing that your suppliers see you in a rosier light than they in fact do. It can be inferred that firms should be wary of proclaiming that they are adopting partnerships with suppliers unless they are sure that actions and behaviour will be consistent. Firms which talk partnership and then continue to use threats and sanctions may find that the chances of effective co-operation become less.

In summary, therefore, whilst much of the prescriptive literature emphasizes the establishment of trusting relationships and focuses on the interface between organizations, the work described here suggests that this may be a difficult task. Nevertheless, effective co-operation may be achieved in terms of integrating the operations of buyers and sellers. However, one of the main barriers to establishing collaboration may lie in the perceived likelihood of the use or abuse of power; a problem that seems to be exacerbated by the careless use of partnership language when actions do not match the rhetoric.

2 Competitive tendering and partnership in the public sector

Andrew Erridge

This chapter examines the selection of and relationships with suppliers in the public sector. The use of competitive tendering and restrictions on close relations with suppliers are imposed largely for reasons of accountability and probity and the application of partnership sourcing to the public sector remains limited. The reasons for this will be examined and an assessment will be made of what features of partnership may be appropriate within various parts of the public sector.

Analysing competition

The characteristics of partnership have been explored fully in the Introduction and Chapter 1. By way of contrast aspects of competition are now analysed. The common characteristics of competitive bidding include closed, fixed-price competitive bidding, short-term, one-off contracts which are almost always awarded on the basis of the lowest price (Slatter 1990 and Spekman 1988); multiple suppliers, detailed contracts and win–lose negotiation (Baily 1987). The traditional argument in support of using competitive bidding is that it enables the buyer to take advantage of competition to obtain the lowest price for his requirements (Dobler et al. 1984, Quayle 1992). It is claimed that the knowledge that a bidder is competing with other firms compels them to quote as low as possible to win the business.

Against competitive bidding, Quayle cites the difficulties, expense and time associated with switching to new suppliers, including the need for new contracts, handling new documents, and developing new procedures. There is a need to weigh the potential benefits from possible price reduction against the increased costs arising from adaptation and establishing new relationships, including quality failure. Moreover, an actual supplier in a competitive situation would have no incentive to avoid poor performance towards the end of the contract, unless it is essential that the business is retained when it is re-tendered.

In summary, the simple dichotomy between competition and partnership masks a considerable degree of complexity in its analysis, and a significant amount of variation in its application.

Constraints on the application of partnership

The main constraint concerning the nature of the relationship between an organization and its suppliers is custom and practice – traditional adversarial practices are maintained despite formal recognition of the benefits of partnership. Thus it is not surprising that the Latham Review (1994) of procurement and contractual relations in the UK construction industry concluded that adversarial contractual attitudes and poor productivity were the most serious problems facing the industry.

Lamming's report for the DTI and Society of Motor Manufacturers and Traders (1994) suggests that there are considerable difficulties in implementing lean supply or partnership in sectors and countries where adversarial relationships have traditionally been dominant. In this respect it may be anticipated that the public sector is unlikely to provide fertile ground for the implementation of partnership. The low regard in which purchasing has traditionally been held in the public sector is ade-

quately captured in its description as an 'administrative cinderella' (Williams and Smellie 1985). The main problem in the
public sector has been to ensure that suppliers are selected not
on the grounds of political expediency, economic survival of
companies, favouritism or fraud, but by transparent procedures
open to audit which give all eligible suppliers an equal opportunity. Hence the emphasis is on ensuring that competitive procedures are followed as part of a process of developing the
professionalism of the purchasing function.

Thus in recent years the UK government has paid considerable attention to the reform and performance of the procurement function, with a series of reports on procurement in central
government (Cabinet Office 1984; Central Unit on Procurement
annual progress reports from 1986; Treasury 1986, 1991, 1993)
and the NHS (Audit Commission 1991; National Audit Office
1991). The main thrust of these reports was to reinforce the
emphasis on competition. At the same time, improved purchasing practice was sought through better organization combining
delegation with clear lines of accountability; professionally
trained, full-time staff; effective information systems; and systematic monitoring of performance. The connection between
efficient procurement and contracting is made in various government publications in relation to contracting out and the purchaser–provider split in the NHS internal market. With the
increased exposure of ministers and senior officials to the financial benefits arising from improved purchasing practice, the
recruitment of purchasing professionals from the private sector,
and the advocacy of the Department of Trade and Industry and
the Central Unit on Procurement (CUP), there has been a greater
recognition of the strategic contribution of improved purchasing
practice. On the one hand this has reinforced formal competitive
tendering but, on the other, it has laid the basis for introducing
best purchasing practice from leading companies in the private
sector, including aspects of partnership.

The White Paper on Government Procurement Strategy
(Treasury 1995) recognized the strategic importance of procurement, together with an increased emphasis on securing the benefits of best purchasing practice. The White Paper advocated a

mixed approach of partnership within competition, designed to meet the specific objectives of the public sector.

Evidence of the application of such a hybrid model in the purchase of supplies is provided by Erridge and Nondi (1994). Its features include supplier selection combining competitive tender with pre- and post-tender negotiation; limited number of suppliers per item; medium-term contract period; fairly formal contractual relations, with guarded but frequent communications with suppliers; a preference for win-win negotiations with suppliers; and a degree of collaboration on joint activities such as materials specification and forecasting, cost reduction, training and research and development. In respect of communications with suppliers and negotiation there is evidence to support the partnership option, suggesting that such practices are not alien to public sector purchasing managers. The research also showed that these purchasing practices invariably result in the achievement of value for money, and operate within accountability requirements.

Legislation and policy on public procurement

Procurement on behalf of central government in Britain is co-ordinated by the CUP, whose role is to provide advice and guidance to government departments. The main purchasing organizations are the Ministry of Defence Procurement Executive; the Central Office of Information; the Buying Agency; the Central Computer and Telecommunications Agency, and the recently privatized Stationery Office. In addition, departments and agencies have their own purchasing staff, and retain budgetary responsibility. In general, departments now have more freedom to set up their own contracts, rather than being tied to those offered by government purchasing organizations. Devolved budgets and agentization under the 'Next Steps' initiative have also increased the competitive and customer-oriented nature of the purchasing process. All these organizations, however, remain subject to the EC public procurement directives, UK regulations, central government guidelines, as well as public accounting rules.

EC public procurement directives

The opening up of public procurement to competition from all member states is an integral part of the European single market. The public procurement directives require that tenders above specified thresholds as well as contract award notices must be advertised in the official journal of the EC. The directives cover procurement of supplies, works and services by public sector contracting authorities as well as utilities, whether in the public or private sector. They provide three ways in which contracts can be awarded:

- open procedure – any supplier may tender
- restricted procedure – any supplier may apply to be considered
- negotiated procedure – direct discussions take place between the purchaser and one or more suppliers of the purchaser's choice.

It is clear that the EC directives reflect the competitive model of procurement. This is particularly evident in the emphasis on formal tendering procedures, attracting bids from a number of suppliers, and maintaining an arm's-length relationship with suppliers. Some flexibility is provided in the selection criteria by the opportunity to specify the most economically advantageous offer rather than lowest price. Implementation of the directives in the UK is monitored by the Treasury, which takes a strong line on ensuring compliance, and requires formal monitoring returns from departments on implementation, thus reinforcing the tendency within departments to 'play it safe' and follow competitive procedures.

Financial accountability

Public procurement involves the expenditure of taxpayers' money and is therefore subject to the same detailed accountability procedures as all public expenditure. The all-pervasive role of the Comptroller and Auditor General backed by the Public

Accounts Committee (PAC) in auditing and scrutinizing the probity of expenditure and value for money is a powerful incentive for departmental accounting officers to ensure that strict procedures are in place to avoid financial irregularity or lack of economy, efficiency and effectiveness in public procurement. Procurement matters have frequently been the subject of accounting officers' appearances before the PAC, reflecting the high risk of fraud and corruption in this area. The effect has been to reinforce mechanisms for reducing the risk of coming to the attention of the PAC. Hence the rules enforcing competitive bidding are a safety device whilst the greater risks associated with partnership would not be welcomed by those who may be held to account.

Value for money

Value for money (VFM) is identified as the main objective for public procurement (CUP 1989). The concept is usually defined by economy, efficiency and effectiveness which have been the basis for government policy since the launch of the Financial Management Initiative (Treasury 1982). It has been argued, however, that a predominantly economizing or cost-cutting approach has been adopted, with at best an emphasis on increasing efficiency by maintaining levels of service with fewer staff and resources (Hartley 1986, Pollitt 1985 and Flynn 1992).

The CUP guidelines stipulate the use of competition as a way of achieving VFM. There is provision in the tendering procedures for holding: (a) pre-tender meetings and consultations with potential bidders to discuss and resolve problems; (b) post-tender negotiations with a few bidders whose bids are attractive in order to negotiate better terms, and (c) debriefing of unsuccessful bidders so that they can know why they were unsuccessful. In evaluation of bids, various factors are considered including ability and creativity of the bidder; commercial, financial, technical aspects; longer-term considerations and the dependability of the bidder. The general principle is that assessment of bids must be systematic, thorough and fair and contract periods for continuing recurrent purchases are flexible, normally between one to three years with provision for revalidation, renegotiation or re-tendering. In deciding on the exact contract period, consideration is given to the need to balance the advantages of competition entailed in short contract periods with advantages of stability entailed in longer-term contracts. Whilst price reduction or avoidance of price increases is identified as the most obvious example of VFM improvement, reflecting an economizing approach, others such as greater quantity and/or improved quality for the same cost, improved delivery or performance, reflect more of an efficiency or effectiveness approach.

Emphasis on price primarily is unlikely to be compatible with a partnership approach, but there is sufficient flexibility in the concept of VFM for a mix of other criteria to be applied. Value for money implies the balanced attainment of the above factors, in that it can be enhanced by increasing or at least assuring quality and on-time delivery of requirements while minimizing total costs. Such a mix could be achieved by a partnership approach, but procedures such as those laid down by the EC directives and the concern for financial accountability would tend to dictate the imposition of rules and procedures which prevent the achievement of value for money in a balanced way.

Competitive tendering for services

The emphasis on competition is equally explicit in relation to services, with practice in government departments and agencies governed by a series of reports and guidance requiring the clear separation of client and contractor and laying down formal tendering procedures to ensure that all bidders are treated equitably (Treasury 1986 and 1991). Conservative governments were particularly concerned to prevent collusion between the client organization and in-house bid teams by introducing strict rules to ensure that private sector bidders were not disadvantaged in terms of the scope of the contract, provision of information or treatment of overhead costs. Such procedures are enforced by legislation in respect of local authorities, and are set out in departmental directives as regards the National Health Service. With the introduction of the EC Services Directive in 1993, the procedures to be followed in the market testing programme for government departments now have legislative backing, and a further legal dimension is added to compulsory competitive tendering (CCT) by local authorities. Thus the climate of competition as a necessary mechanism for facilitating government policy on contracting out of services clearly reinforces the emphasis on the use of competitive tendering in respect of goods.

Contracting for local authority services has been enforced by successive Local Government Acts (1980, 1988 and 1992). The 1980 Act covered construction, buildings and highways services, and a rate of return to be achieved was specified. From 1988 contracting was extended to building and street cleaning, catering, grounds maintenance and vehicle repair, and to the maintenance of sport and leisure facilities in the following year. The 1992 Act dealt with professional services, including administrative, legal, financial, personnel and computing. This Act also specified time periods for each stage in the tendering process, and introduced restrictions on the costs offset against in-house bids. These measures were thought necessary in order to ensure that outside bidders were not disadvantaged by having insufficient time to prepare bids, nor by their bids being made on a less favourable cost basis than that of the in-house team.

Arguments for and against contracting out of services revolve largely around the issue of whether they should continue to be provided directly by the public sector or should be contracted out to the private sector. Arguments in favour of direct provision include the maintenance of values such as citizen participation, equity, access for the poor and minorities; and the maintenance of a wider range and higher quality of service provision for social reasons than a judgement based purely on what the market would allow. In practice, however, the majority of local authority and health service contracts subjected to competitive tendering have been awarded to in-house bids.

The wider political issue of whether services should be provided by the public or private sectors is of less significance to the theme of this chapter than whether competitive tendering is an efficient and effective way of letting service contracts, in preference to a partnership approach. An important part of the answer to this question is whether the financial savings and improved value for money arising from the market testing or competitive tendering process outweigh the additional transaction costs incurred in the process of contracting. Chaundy and Uttley (1993) provide evidence in respect of local authority refuse collection services that average gross savings from competitive tendering of 22 per cent were achieved. Similar savings are reported in research elsewhere in the UK (Hartley and Huby 1985; Audit Commission 1989) and in the USA (Morgan and England 1988 and Rehfuss 1991). The average increased costs of organizing and administering CCT were 4.6 per cent of winning tender values. They conclude that administrative costs of implementing CCT do not outweigh savings obtained from competition. Furthermore, the assumption that only competitive tendering incurs transaction costs is mistaken. The negotiation of partnership relationships is recognized as being very expensive in terms of the time of senior managers, and may be almost as demanding in terms of paperwork if detailed proposals and expectations of both partners are to be documented.

Chaundy and Uttley (1993) also provide evidence that in the majority of authorities service quality has improved, which is a benefit often claimed for partnership relationships but not recognized as a necessary concomitant of competitive tendering. Improved management and organization is identified as a main contributor to cost improvement, together with revised working practices, changed conditions of service and reduction in manpower.

Other benefits of the contracting process which will not necessarily arise from a partnership approach are the clarification of service requirements in terms of quantity, quality and cost; a greater focus on the recipient of public services as a customer; more active, hands-on management and monitoring of service delivery; and greater transparency about the costs of central administrative and support services. Only if the client and prospective partner go through a similar process of detailed specification of needs and customer service levels, analysis of costs and management and monitoring arrangements, and the client has means other than competitive bidding of testing the market for suppliers, are similar benefits likely to arise. It is argued therefore that competition resulting in the award of service contracts to either public or private sector providers, as a means of replacing less efficient and effective direct delivery through public sector hierarchies, is more likely to achieve the government's strategic objectives than partnership, which could simply see cosy public monopolies continuing as direct service organizations or transferred to the private sector.

The partnership within competition theme of the White Paper on Government Procurement Strategy (Treasury 1995) is restated in respect of large service contracts. It indicates that whilst contracts will continue to be awarded on the basis of tenders, features compatible with partnership are identified. These include discussion of specifications with suppliers to take advantage of their expertise and encourage innovation; longer-term contract durations; sharing of risks; and promoting continuous improvement in performance through incentive contracts with the sharing of benefits. To what extent procurement staff, especially those in local authorities, will be able or encouraged to apply such practices within the constraints of legislation, rules on accountability and probity, and competitive tendering procedures is, however, a matter for conjecture.

Internal market for healthcare and social services

The internal market for healthcare and social services represented a significant extension of service contracting into the provision of professional services previously provided by hospitals and social services units within the NHS hierarchy. Ancillary services within the NHS, including domestic, cleaning, catering, buildings and grounds maintenance, had been subjected to competitive tendering since 1983. The aims of the internal market were to introduce competition into the provision of health and social services care; to open health and social services to market-based providers; to delegate budgets to provider unit managers and thereby create incentives to reduce costs and improve efficiency; and to increase consumer choice.

In parallel with the client–contractor split in respect of contracting in central and local government, there is a clear split between purchaser and provider. Purchasers are the district health authorities, general practitioner fund holders (GPFHs) and local authority social services departments. Providers are a mixture of NHS trusts, directly managed units (DMUs) which remain part of the NHS hierarchy, voluntary bodies and private sector providers.

Several problems arise with this approach. There is an absence of genuine competition in some services and regions, with the vast majority of healthcare treatments provided by trusts and DMUs, although it was anticipated that competition between trusts and with private hospitals would develop over time. Whether this will result in the closure of 'inefficient' providers is likely to remain more of a political than an economic decision, especially where there are no suitable alternative providers for those services designated as 'local', such as accident and emergency. There is a greater degree of competition for some social services, where voluntary bodies and private companies are heavily involved in providing care in the community. There are also rigorous statutory requirements, especially in respect of social services, which makes market entry difficult for new service providers.

Moreover, current contracts reflect historical patterns of service provision and therefore resource allocation (Harrison 1993), and purchasers are not allowed to alter providers' contracts by more than 10 per cent from year to year. At present there is a lack of reliable cost information on which to base contract pricing, especially in respect of buildings, support and ancillary services which were previously regarded as 'free'.

The purchasing process follows the typical contracting cycle, with specification of needs, submission of bids in the form of business plans, evaluation, negotiation and award of contracts. However, given the distortions of the market, the competitive aspect of this process is limited. Providers know roughly what the resources allocated to purchasers for various services will be, and that they are guaranteed a high proportion of the business awarded in the previous contract. Block contracts for volumes of services are mainly used, rather than the more precise cost per case or cost and volume contracts. The scope for competition on price is heavily constrained, and therefore other aspects, such as service quality, are emphasized. Specification of levels and quality of service to be provided within health and social services is, however, problematical, especially in terms of outcomes (Kerrison 1993). At present the transaction costs of the process of drawing up detailed specifications, strategic and business plans are high in relation to any cost and service improvements achieved. There is also an absence of the skills required in managing the contracting process and monitoring performance in respect of both purchasers and providers, with most managers given responsibility for contracting having no previous procurement experience.

The Labour government elected in May 1997 is committed to ending the internal market because of its increased administrative costs and its effect of disadvantaging patients of non-fund-holding GPs (Manifesto). Whilst no detailed plans have been announced at the time of writing, Frank Dobson, the Secretary of State for Health, advocated moving from one year to longer-term contracts and 'cutting down on the flow of invoices' in a speech to staff of the NHS Management Executive (Leeds, 9 May 1997). The Manifesto also states that the 'purchasing and provision of care are necessary and distinct functions and will remain so' and that GPs will move from fundholding to commissioning. Thus it appears that the principle of purchasing within the NHS will remain. Whilst there will clearly be changes of emphasis and process, the historically close relationships and shared culture between purchasers and providers has facilitated more of a partnership approach which the new government's proposals reinforce.

The formal, arm's-length competitive tendering process prescribed for ancillary services, which is largely incompatible with the trust and long-term relationships essential for partnership, does not apply. Instead, details of service levels and quality are negotiated, and monitoring of performance is a joint process supported by the health and social services professionals' peer review processes. It may be anticipated that provider trusts, especially acute hospitals, will increasingly offer innovation and expertise in specialist treatments and collaborate with purchasing authorities on cost improvement activities.

Economic and social policy objectives

Consideration of the strategic merits of competitive and partnership methods of procurement in the public sector needs to take into account the fact that public procurement may also be used to promote other general economic and social objectives of government policy. Health and social care services provide an example where the market's emphasis on price and efficiency must be tempered by the values of equity and access to service provision, as well as the avoidance of political embarrassment.

The perceived failures of public procurement have produced a body of literature on the economics of forms of contract (McAfee and McMillan 1988; Jones 1997), with criticism of the cost plus contracts traditionally used. Such practices, whilst clearly wasteful from a competitive perspective, may be quite rational if the objective is to use taxpayers' money to sustain jobs and protect national champions. There is evidence, however, that the effect of such cosy relationships over a lengthy period of time is a decline in the competitiveness of the companies reliant on government contracts

In the USA explicit preference is given to small firms and ethnic minorities in assessing bids for public contracts, whilst in the UK means of supporting small firms, workshops for the disabled and a concern for environmentally friendly procurement are reflected in CUP guidance. Heinritz et al. (1991) state that the government's use of public procurement as an instrument of social policy (e.g. preferences to small business, minority groups, designated regions etc.) often acts as a restriction on the buying officer's ability to place business in a competitive manner and in a sense conflicts with the overall objectives of the procurement process.

There will always be a political dimension to public procurement due to its significance in terms of public expenditure, the performance of national or local industry, and the desire of politicians for re-election. Whilst ministers and local politicians may espouse the virtues of open competition, and practise it openly where key interests are not threatened, in large contracts, such as for defence equipment, political influence will be paramount, even if it is only reflected in the requirement in placing a contract with a foreign supplier that a high proportion of work should be subcontracted to domestic companies. In this context, partnership concepts such as non-competitive selection, single-source supply, informal contractual relations and very extensive joint activities with suppliers seem to carry increased risks of political influence and the predominance of other economic and social objectives.

By contrast, formal competitive procedures may be introduced in order to restrict the scope of local politicians to use the award of contracts to companies as a means of local economic development. Similarly client managers engaged in the competitive tendering of services in central or local government or the NHS are constrained by detailed competitive procedures designed to ensure that in-house bids are not given undue preference. Adoption of partnership concepts in these contexts could easily lead to the cosy, anti-competitive practices partnership sourcing justifiably seeks to avoid.

How different is the public sector?

The assumption underlying much of the above discussion is that the public sector in some ways is different from the private sector. However, private sector companies are accountable to shareholders who may pursue a quick return on their investment, which could make them less amenable to the long-term building of relationships with suppliers implied by partnership. In large companies there may be the same kind of detailed accounting and auditing procedures designed to protect against potential fraud in the public sector, reinforcing the reliance on formal competitive procedures. There is evidence that support for national and local suppliers is not unique to the public sector.

What is distinctive about the public sector is the imposition across all public sector organizations of competitive bidding procedures via EC legislation and government policy; the requirement to apply competitive tendering for all services, including 'white-collar' services such as accounting, traditionally provided in-house; the emphasis on procedural probity rather than effectiveness of policy imposed through audit and the Public Accounts Committee. These suggest the necessity for a competitive bidding approach.

The context is also distinctive in that there is pressure on and from government ministers to take decisions for non-commercial reasons. The 'political' dimension of procurement may not be entirely absent from the private sector, in that chairmen and directors may take decisions on specific contracts in line with the overall direction of the company's future business: development of new markets or technology may be assisted by short-term uncompetitive purchases from particular countries or companies. But the 'political' dimension in public procurement is much more extensive, so that pressures to override purchasing decisions on political grounds may arise at any time from local or national political parties and their representatives, business interests, employee representatives and even other governments. Thus whilst detailed competitive procedures may be enforced in public sector organizations, their outcomes, or the procedures themselves, may at any time be ignored or overridden on political grounds. In this context partnership concepts may provide the pretext for the development or maintenance of closed, anti-competitive corporatist relationships.

Conclusion

Public sector competition is embodied in legislation, formal rules and procedures designed to ensure as far as possible the proper use of public funds, the achievement of value for money, and that potential suppliers are not discriminated against. In particular, the European Community's directives on public procurement and UK legislation on compulsory competitive tendering lay down formal procedures requiring selection by competitive tendering in most cases. Such procedures, and the penalties associated with non-compliance, have tended to result in a reluctance to get too close to suppliers, and therefore made difficult any attempt to achieve the claimed benefits of partnership relations in the public sector. In some respects partnership may be undesirable. There is an increased risk that, in the absence of genuine market mechanisms, political interference, collusion between budget holders and suppliers and fraud will result, against which competitive tendering was introduced to provide protection.

However, the hybrid model of partnership within competition would seem appropriate for the public sector, combining open competitive tendering with transparent criteria and procedures for selecting suppliers. During the period of the contract, partnership may be actively developed, with an emphasis on continuously improving the quality of the goods and services delivered to internal or external customers. In the case of the general public, or particular client groups such as the disabled, constituting the final customer, a commitment from partnership suppliers to the 'public service ethic' of equity, accessibility and fairness will need to be present alongside a commitment to drive cost down and quality up. Whilst the partnership supplier could not be guaranteed winning the contract on retendering, they would clearly be in a strong position to do so. The prospects for genuine competition could be maintained by the contracting authority splitting contracts between two or three suppliers, and encouraging new suppliers to come into the market. Thus the public sector's strategic objectives of compliance and accountability could be assured, whilst improved relationships with suppliers and more competitive supply markets should ensure that value for money is enhanced.

Further reading

Audit Commission (1989), 'Preparing for compulsory competition', occasional paper no. 7, January.

Audit Commission (1991), 'Improving the supplies service in the NHS: a report for the NHS Management Executive, Department of Health.

Baily P. (1987), *Purchasing and Supply Management*, Chapman and Hall, London.

Cabinet Office (1984), *Government Purchasing*, HMSO, London.

Central Unit on Procurement (1989), 'Supplement to CUP newsletter,' H.M. Treasury, HMSO, London, Summer.

Chaundy, D., and Uttley, M. (1993), 'The economics of compulsory competitive tendering: issues, evidence and the case of municipal refuse collection', *Public Policy and Administration*, vol. 8, no. 2, Summer, pp. 25–41.

Dobler, D.W., Lee, L. and Burt, D.N. (1984), *Purchasing and Materials Management*, McGraw-Hill, New York.

Erridge, A. and Nondi, R. (1994), 'Public procurement: partnership and competition,' *European Journal of Purchasing and Supply Management*, vol. 1, no. 3, pp. 169–79.

Flynn, N. (1992), *Public Sector Management*, Harvester Wheatsheaf, Hemel Hempstead.

Harrison, A. (1993), 'NHS healthcare services' in Harrison, A. (ed.), *From Hierarchy to Contract*, Policy Journals, Hermitage, nr. Newbury.

Hartley, K. and Huby, M. (1985), 'Contracting out in health and local authorities: prospects, progress and pitfalls,' *Public Money*, vol. 5, no. 2, pp. 23–26.

Hartley, K. (1986), 'Value for money in defence,' *Public Money*, March, pp. 33–38.

Heinritz, S., Farrell, P.V., Giunipero, L. and Kolchin, M. (1991), *Purchasing Principles and Applications*, Prentice-Hall, New York.

Jones, G.L. (1997), 'The impact of regulatory legislation on contractual risk and the form of contracts used in the UK and Republic of Ireland, *European Journal of Purchasing and Supply Management*, vol. 3, no. 3, pp. 137–46.

Kerrison, S. (1993), 'Contracting and the quality of medical care' in Tilley, I. (ed.), *Managing the Internal Market*, Paul Chapman, London.

Lamming, R.C. (1994), 'Review of relationships between vehicle manufacturers and suppliers', Department of Trade and Industry/Society of Motor Manufacturers and Traders, London, February.

Latham, M. (1994), *Constructing the Team: Review of Procurement and Contractual Relations in the UK Construction Industry*, HMSO, London.

McAfee, R. and McMillan, J. (1988), *Incentives in Government Contracts*, University of Toronto Press.

Morgan, D.R. and England, R.E. (1988), 'The two faces of privatisation,' *Public Administration Review*, November/December, pp. 979–987.

National Audit Office (1991), 'Health Service Supplies in England', Comptroller and Auditor General.

Pollitt, C. (1985), 'Measuring performance: a new system for the National Health Service', *Policy and Politics*, vol. 13, no. 1, pp. 1–16.

Quayle, M. (1992), 'Developing industrial purchasing policy,' *Purchasing and Supply Management Journal*, February, pp. 27–30.

Rehfuss, J. (1991), 'The competitive agency: thoughts from contracting out in Great Britain and the United States', *International Review of Administrative Studies*, vol. 5, pp. 465–482.

Slatter, S. (1990), 'Strategic marketing variables under conditions of competitive bidding', *Strategic Management Journal*, vol. 11, no. 4, pp. 309–317.

Spekman, R.E. (1988), 'Strategic supplier selection: understanding longterm buyer relationships', *Business Horizons*, vol. 31, no. 4, July/August, pp. 75–81.

Treasury (1982), 'Efficiency and effectiveness in the Civil Service: government observations on the third report from the Treasury and Civil Service Committee,' Cmnd. 8616, HMSO, London.

Treasury (1986), 'Using private enterprise in government,' HMSO, London.

Treasury, (1990), The Government's Expenditure Plans 1990–91 to 1992–3, Chapter 1 Ministry of Defence, Cm 1001, HMSO: London.

Treasury (1991), 'Competing for quality,' Cm 1730, HMSO, London.

Treasury (1993), 'Organisation of procurement in government departments and their agencies,' HMSO, London.

Treasury (1995), 'Setting new standards: a strategy for government procurement,' HMSO, London.

Williams, R. and Smellie, R. (1985), 'Public Purchasing: an administrative cinderella,' *Public Administration*, Spring, pp. 22–39.

3 The automotive industry – the customer's perspective: a study of the Rover Group

Garry B Grove,
Production Purchasing Director, Rover Group

In the early 1980s Rover recognized that a lack of centralized purchasing combined with a traditional approach to sourcing had resulted in the following:

- price-based sourcing with inadequate knowledge of supplier capabilities in terms of manufacturing and total business performance
- proliferation of suppliers
- strained relationships and a lack of meaningful communication with suppliers
- a primarily confrontational purchasing environment
- outmoded process controls and an over-reliance on inspection-based systems
- decisions being made in functional isolation.

At the same time, the company's own processes for delivery and implementation of new products to the market were flawed in a number of areas. The product engineering and manufacturing functions were not in harmony and the notoriety of a design challenge being 'passed over the wall' to its eventual maker, without prior consultation or involvement as to whether it was fit for purpose, was a common experience.

This chapter outlines how these challenges were faced, the changes made and the benefits achieved.

Strategic influences in the delivery of change within partnership relations at Rover – 'The Rover Way'

During 1990 Rover Purchasing developed its own research and response, entitled 'Rover Tomorrow', to the dynamic challenge and pressures facing European vehicle producers. This outlined the threat to established European producers of a Japanese transplant capability within a market suffering from over capacity. Since the early 1990s recessionary impact combined with increasing vehicle feature content had constrained pricing activity in key world markets. The addition of emission limits and safety-related improvements (e.g. air bag, side intrusion beams, security systems), in parallel with the need to introduce aggressive customer incentivizing programmes, further weakened pricing and ultimately profit opportunity for automotive producers.

Rover developed a pro-active, vision-driven strategy which allowed it to anticipate rather than react to these developments. Its purchasing strategies, in particular, aimed at achieving 'world class' standards of performance in its supply base, were tied into the wider strategic company influences, as follows.

Simultaneous engineering and the role of the supplier

In the past, suppliers were selected predominantly on price competitiveness resulting from a competitive enquiry or post-tender completion of the intellectual design effort by Rover engineers. From the mid-1980s, the early nomination of key suppliers changed the nature of supplier selection, working relationships and their interface with Rover's business processes. Suppliers of strategic importance were selected at the concept stage to influence engineering design and technology and ultimately product quality, by providing technical input, manufacturing process and project management strengths. This product development approach to harnessing supplier expertise, knowledge and technology, demanded early involvement of capable businesses in the design process, together with transparent cost management techniques.

To identify suppliers capable of supporting this activity, it became essential to measure their total business performance (TBP). This required a radically different method of suppliers' evaluation. To meet this need, Rover developed RG 2000 (1991) which was based on the Kaizen or continuous improvement philosophy (see Imai 1986).

RG 2000 business model – supplier evaluation and diagnostic assessment

The RG 2000 business specification created the TBP model which focused upon all elements of supplier capability and support services. It was prevention based, analysing total company strengths and weaknesses, placing further emphasis upon strategic alliance with suppliers and development of the supply chain. It introduced the platform for developing strategic supplier partnerships through objective measurement and diagnostic assessment of improvement needs.

Total quality improvement

In 1987 a total quality initiative was embarked upon, the aim of which was to provide extraordinary customer satisfaction at the lowest achievable cost in relation to products. To move forward with the principles of total quality improvement (TQI), the Rover Group and its suppliers needed to establish robust measures for evaluating performance and improvement. Historically, the company had assessed its suppliers on the basis of their quality management systems and had given importance to advanced quality planning (AQP), process control and 'in service' warranty performance. RG 2000 was designed as a continuation of AQP. It defined minimum business requirements, emphasized strategic areas which were often overlooked and encouraged both ownership and flexibility in achieving common business goals.

In addition to requiring supplier registration to the ISO 9000 series, the Rover Group placed great importance on assessing suppliers' attitudes and plans towards employee involvement, teamworking and the embodiment of a genuine total quality philosophy. The company also sought to understand how suppliers determined their corporate/business strategy and organized their businesses to satisfy customers' requirements and expectations. Equally important was the need for the company and its suppliers to continuously review their business relationship with regard to management, longer-term planning, cost reduction and efficiency improvement.

During 1993 RG 2000 was increased in scope and sophistication to concentrate upon key business metrics as a natural progression towards world-class benchmarks. Supplier excellence awards were also introduced to enable supplier performance and improvement achievements to be formally recognized. Recognition of year-on-year improvement targets were based upon RG 2000 data in addition to plant performance measures of supply and quality parts per million (ppm) statistics.

Rover Group quality strategy – the supplier implications

Rover's quality strategy was developed through an extensive review of all company processes and stated the company's vision, mission and critical success factors (CSFs). This significant step provided alignment to the company's corporate vision but also facilitated planning in all supporting areas of Rover, including the development of a purchasing quality strategy.

Purchasing quality strategy

The purchasing quality strategy, as a strategic arm of the company's corporate goals, defined key processes for full optimization of the supply chain and identified milestones essential to the achievement and delivery of the plan. The relationship between the quality strategy and purchasing quality strategy is shown in Figure 3.1. The purchasing quality strategy was founded upon the following key business processes:

- supplier reduction (rationalization)

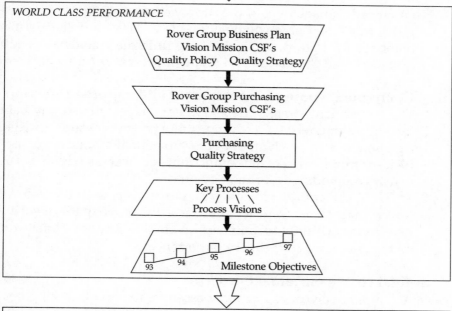

THE VISION

Rover is internationally renowned for extraordinary customer satisfaction.

THE MISSION

Rover Group's business is to produce and sell distinctive and desirable vehicles known for their robustness and driver appeal. Our aim is continually to improve our products and services, to satisfy our customers and make a profit. This will allow us to prosper as a business to the benefit of our customers, dealers, suppliers, shareholders and employees alike.

WORLD CLASS PERFORMANCE

Rover Group Business Plan
Vision Mission CSF's
Quality Policy   Quality Strategy

Rover Group Purchasing
Vision Mission CSF's

Purchasing
Quality Strategy

Key Processes
Process Visions

Milestone Objectives
93 94 95 96 97

ROVER GROUP PURCHASING VISION AND MISSION

Purchasing's aim is to provide world-class products and services at the lowest total cost in support of Rover's commitment to extraordinary customer satisfaction.

We are committed to excellence, through investment in our people, added value working, and constancy of purpose. By proactively developing supplier partnerships which are world competitive, we will secure preferred customer status.

Figure 3.1   Relationship between quality strategy and purchasing quality strategy

- component strategy development and supplier selection
- supplier development
- total cost management
- people development (involvement, development, training)
- business planning
- leadership.

Supplier reduction

The strategy aimed for a chain consisting of 400 or less suppliers. The advantages of concentrated development improvement and common understanding which flowed from this were vital to enhanced management of the supply chain. Selecting these suppliers was based on a combination of RG 2000, supplier performance evaluation within the business units, new model selection decisions, and the nature and scope of present relationships.

Component strategy development and supplier selection

The component strategy development shaped the supply base for future models by creating strategy core groups (SCGs). Agreement was reached, via cross-functional teams, on a supplier grouping for specific components or systems within a particular commodity or technology type.

The most critical elements of purchasing and the role of Rover's suppliers were featured at a micro planning level by milestones within the purchasing quality strategy. Total cost management was of primary importance.

Total cost management process

A competitively priced product essential to success in all global markets is dependent upon a minimum total cost approach to material content.

Rover recognized that the ability to deliver a competitively priced, quality product to the market place profitably, depended upon a solid foundation of variable cost from initial concept through to series production volume. This in itself was not a startlingly new revelation, but the introduction of effective cost management (ECM) techniques that could realize the crucial objective called for the development, introduction and adoption of a new process. ECM moved the new product introduction process from the traditional approach of costing the design to designing to cost targets for a new model proposal.

Based on market evaluation of price and product positioning, a target selling price for a new product offering was translated beyond Rover's own 'added value' operating costs to a material (or variable) vehicle cost target. Synthetic vehicle component (or system) costs could then be identified and broken down to constituent part level for which individual design solutions could then be developed. Existing vehicle or competitor product benchmark comparisons also aided this process of developing realistic cost targets. The significance of variable costs which accounted for 65–70 per cent of a vehicle's eventual cost, demanded robust control and was crucial to making a profit once a car was in production. The identified concept cost targets had to be achieved over a product introduction cycle that was typically 36 months in duration.

The principles of ECM within the new product introduction (NPI) process were:

- Designing to a cost.
- Suppliers were fully integrated members of the 'core team'. The core team was the multidisciplinary project management team responsible for the introduction of a specific component design. A core team consisted of the component product engineer, the buyer, manufacturing engineer, technical support (purchasing quality engineer), logistics and support areas, where necessary, and of course the strategic supplier. Core teams established the initial concept component cost targets.
- Cost transparency (or open book). This was derived from a quotation analysis form (QAF) which broke down the component cost into constituent elements, in addition to capital investment costs or supplier tooling.
- Cost understanding. This was developed prior to any programme approval stage or real commitment to expenditure occurred.
- Best practice. The strategy was applied at the concept design

stage and throughout project management and was largely focused upon the process of manufacture.

- Cost reviews. These were held at each critical key event milestone or build phase within the process of introduction, ensuring that change management impact was fully measured.

The responsibilities of both Rover and her suppliers in ECM are summarized below:

Rover	*Supplier*
Suppliers were both enrolled and committed to cost targets.	Cost targets were jointly agreed but not imposed.
Component designs were geared towards optimum cost.	Design/Engineering expertise was able to influence the product and costs.
A disciplined process for management of project costs existed.	Focus was upon cost rather than supplier margins.
Products were profitable.	Profitable new products.

Best practice

The philosophy of best practice was allied to continuous improvement and the aim was to eliminate waste. Typical key areas for elimination of waste and cost proved to be:

- material yield
- material specification
- machine layout
- transportation
- material flow and process layout
- inventory reduction
- design change improvement.

The objective of best practice was to be pro-active in assisting suppliers to become 'best in class'. It sought to optimize the processes involved in the manufacture and delivery of a product to ensure total quality at the lowest cost, by the elimination of waste. Rover recognised that through working with suppliers their own competitiveness in the market place could be improved along with that of the supply chain. The effectiveness of suppliers' manufacturing techniques was optimized through early involvement at the vehicle concept stage. Utilizing suppliers specialist knowledge helped to ensure that parts were designed for ease of manufacture and at minimum total cost.

When the initiative of best practice was first introduced, the supply base was sceptical. They saw Rover as knowing best and the idea of 'open book' was not trusted. Gradually, with reassurance and explanation, the suppliers realised that it was a total culture change and Rover meant what they said.

'Rover Tomorrow' strategy

Together with ECM and best practice, 'Rover Tomorrow' formed the key thrust to the Rover supply base in embracing the principles of lean manufacture and supply.

The first version, launched to suppliers during the third quarter of 1991, outlined the concepts of strategic partnership. Its objectives were to build upon the strategic transformation in relationships and to provide a clear vision of Rover's aims in the drive for continuous improvement. The second version was launched one year later and concentrated upon four key areas: quality; cost; logistics and response time; and product change and innovation (see Figure 3.2). It also included a section devoted to the tools and techniques essential to effect step change improvement and methods by which such achievement had been realized within Rover and specific suppliers.

The third version took the programme a step further by presenting details of Rover's world-class benchmarking activity. This focused upon specific business effectiveness measures (BEMs) drawn from RG 2000. Again, the objectives were to continue the partnership theme and promote further understanding with suppliers towards true integration.

Figure 3.2   'Rover Tomorrow' strategy

The fourth version provided further details of the principles of improvement plans based upon the BEMs as they related to an individual supplier's business performance. The importance of external suppliers meant that the company's commitment to achieve world-class levels of performance depended crucially upon the creation of a 'world-class' supplier base and supply chain.

The programme for development of the supplier base was geared towards the achievement of 'world-class' performance using benchmarking techniques to measure and close the competitive gap. The central core of the 'Rover Tomorrow' programme and the overt philosophy that underpinned the purchasing strategies outlined in this chapter was the commitment to work with the supply base to achieve 'world-class' levels of performance. The company did not present suppliers with unexplained cost improvement targets that lacked realism or interest in the long-term survival of the supplier's business. Moreover, they took great strides to share its vision, tools and techniques and develop methodologies of realizing lean production with the supply base.

Closing the competitive gap

The RG 2000 survey gave Rover a detailed understanding of its suppliers' operations and a subsequent agenda for supplier development. This approach lacked, however, the means to quickly take the immediate 'temperature' of a supplier and across different product ranges, benchmark performance.

Around this time surveys were published (A.T. Kearney (1992), and Arthur Anderson (1993)) that claimed a competitive gap of approximately 20 per cent existed between UK suppliers and their Japanese counterparts. This finding was based on a fairly limited survey which needed significant expansion to have universal acceptance. Therefore, against a background of seeking quick and easy supplier measures, a desire to benchmark suppliers to spread best practice and a feeling that a UK–Japanese gap existed, business effectiveness measures were born. They sought to measure those areas that reflected supplier performance, without having so many that focus could not be easily applied. A seventeen-point questionnaire survey was developed supported by working examples, which measured performance across five key areas:

- product quality – measured areas like ppm and time spent in rework
- inventory management – covered stockturns, finished goods stock and work-in-progress
- value chain management – the depth and control of supplier tiers two and three
- equipment effectiveness – studied the management of capital assets, the amount of machinery 'up time' and unplanned non-productive time
- total quality people management – measures of employee involvement, workplace attendance and involuntary staff turnover.

Rover's purchasing team worked with its strategic suppliers to complete the questionnaire, covering 220 suppliers, which represented 73 per cent of the bought-out spend. The BEM database, which is regularly updated, is used to focus on where suppliers have a particular weakness and allowed the improvement to be measured and costed. It allows benchmarking for suppliers across different products, sizes and geographies. In the future it will be used as an essential tool in supplier development and selection and as Rover moves into the late 1990s to compare its supplier base with that of its parent, BMW. This has been developed into a Quality of Service Database (QSDB) for all strategic suppliers' performance measurement.

Distribution efficiency

The opportunities for differential advantages based on product attributes of quality, technology and price is gradually receding as the rest of the world catches up and improves upon the technical and process knowhow that has underpinned much of the industrial success in the West. There are, nevertheless, opportunities to create differential advantages in terms of time based competition as exemplified by the Rover Group's logistics strategy. This strategy seeks to maintain competitiveness in product-based competencies whilst focusing attention on development and improvement of customer service. The key elements of this strategy are to:

- develop the capability to provide a reliable delivery promise to the customer
- achieve a significant reduction in working capital across the total supply chain.

The objective is to focus the entire supply chain on the provision of customer satisfaction, whilst protecting margins by achieving significant cost reduction through the optimization of inventory across the whole supply system. Currently the company satisfies most of its orders by supplying customers from stocks of finished vehicles with resultant difficulties in supply and reaction to customer demands. The new strategy can only be meaningfully supported if production programmes are closely matched to short-term customer demands by establishing a build-to-order capability.

Developments in this direction in the part were thwarted by the vast number of suppliers involved at the first tier. The first-tier supply base is now being reduced by sourcing new business only to those suppliers with whom Rover intends to have a long-term relationship. This is further complemented through a strategy that seeks to source generic families of parts for a model from the same supplier. Secondary and tertiary suppliers will typically be managed by the primary supplier. This strategy has distinct advantages of lower support costs and more responsive suppliers who have a much larger business involvement with the company.

In parallel with the above, there is a commitment at all levels of the company to improve flexibility and quality in supply processes at the product design stage. Suppliers are required to work simultaneously with Rover project teams and to promote:

- the use of common parts across all vehicle derivatives
- the use of carryover blueprint designs, provided they meet the guidelines for flexibility
- planning for volume flexibility through laying down capacity for maximum and minimum volumes
- mix flexibility of variety parts ensuring that all-mix scenarios can be delivered
- genuine customer perceived variety without incurring product complexity through ensuring that all features are independent of each other.

These techniques help to develop products which contribute positively to the company's business objectives as well as technical excellence. The idea is to focus on the delivery of a design which is compatible to the requirements of the supply chain and which can only be achieved through a consistent and clear understanding of the company's objectives across the entire supply chain.

Relationship transformation – building bridges and developing trust

In working closely with its suppliers, meaningful and effective relationships have started to be established. Figure 3.3 demonstrates the areas of culture change taking place through the catalyst of supplier development.

Building such relationships depends fundamentally upon a common business environment founded on trust and integrity. Whilst the concept of business in perpetuity is not contractually defined or stated, the intention is that strategic partnerships should grow and evolve.

The competition will not stand still and what is excellence today will be the common standard tomorrow. This must be firmly recognized within the supply industry to ensure that partnerships do not breed complacency. Suppliers should not feel threatened by benchmarking and comparative analysis techniques; they are vital to continuous improvement. Cost transparency is a mechanism for mutual identification of both improvement in the supply chain and recognition of supplier capabilities by the customer. Rover will not operate the open-book approach to limit suppliers' profits, but it will expect gen-

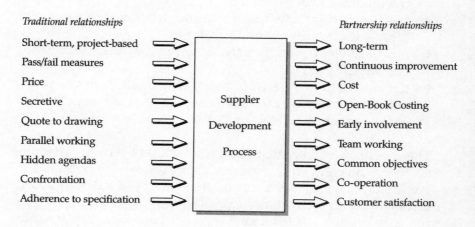

Figure 3.3   A strategic transformation

uine business improvement to be shared. RG 2000, best practice and BEM, are essential components in the development of this strategic transformation and provide the framework for successful partnership (see Figure 3.4).

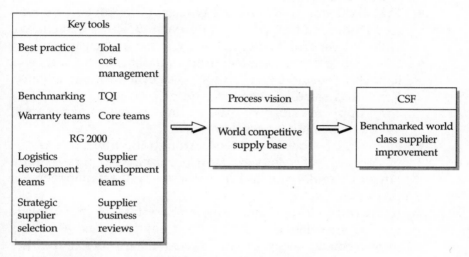

Figure 3.4   Supplier development process vision

Benefits, obstacles and progress

The benefits and rewards from the establishment of effective relationships between supplier and customer manifest themselves in the following business areas:

- Continuous improvements to which there is joint commitment will ultimately realize increased competitiveness. Year-on-year improvement plans will yield opportunities for all customers if harnessed within the total business entity, not with a single customer.
- A shared strategic vision will enable medium- and long-range planning actions to be implemented. Commitment to capital planning programmes, recruitment and training of people can

be resourced in preparation or demand the redeployment of resources. A formal business review structure communicates and exchanges vital information that may otherwise, because it is invisible inside an adversarial relationship, have a potentially catastrophic impact on both parties.

- Cost reduction and business efficiency improvements realized through a best practice approach which, when shared, will increase profitability to both supplier and customer.
- Business growth results from supplier reduction and increased business opportunity within a strategic alliance. Rover has steadily been offering growth of business to its core suppliers as its own product improvements have generated new business in world markets.
- Design excellence is achieved through the utilization of the design and technology expertise of suppliers as part of simultaneous engineering and robustness of project management processes.
- Improved self-understanding also results from suppliers gaining knowledge of their own strengths, weaknesses and improvement needs from customer diagnostics and closer working relationships.

In any business relationship there are impediments to progress. If a strategic alliance is not appropriately structured or insufficiently managed it can bring problems rather than benefits, in particular:

- Loss of leverage or influence can become a main business constraint if a supplier is not enlightened or fully committed to the partnership approach. Hence selection of the right partners and application of the most appropriate sourcing strategy is critical. Rover has committed itself to the pattern of two or more strategic partners in specific component or technology types where the formative stages of partnership or the need for competitive tension has to be observed.
- Technology stagnation or a lack of ongoing investment in research and development may lead a supplier who has best-in-class engineering and product today to be overtaken

tomorrow. If Rover suppliers fail to provide technology developments then the partnership will fail.

- Limits upon achievement in general terms may result if continuous improvement is not practised. Currently there are real areas of concern in supply chain development (beyond the first tier) of the company's strategic suppliers and indeed the industry as a whole.
- 'Low aim is a crime' and if the sights are set too low in not developing the right strategic alliance the achievement of better results from more capable suppliers upon the journey to 'world class' may be frustrated by those moving at a slower pace of change.

The way forward – Rover and its suppliers

In continuing to foster the relationships developed with its strategic suppliers through the initiatives outlined above, Rover will intensify its focus toward the extended enterprise. This will further embrace the customer-led drive towards excellence both in its dealer network, with JIT distribution efficiency improving outbound finished vehicle supply to customers, and in terms of inbound supply of components, materials and services.

Through business effectiveness measures established to close the gap towards 'world class', it has been shown that the first-tier suppliers have an average of 90 suppliers within their own supply chain forming the second tier. This implies approximately 36,000 companies upon whom Rover is dependent in the process of satisfying its customers with quality, reliability and competitiveness. If Rover is to maintain successful growth, the culture of continuous improvement must be inculcated within the supply chain.

Learning and adoption of all the tools, techniques and processes which have generated major improvements to date, is an imperative not merely for Rover and the automotive industry, but also for industry in the UK and Europe. Supplier learning is assisted by the formation of Rover Learning Business (RLB), which was established as a separate learning company within Rover in the early 1990s. The aims of RLB are to further learn by providing the necessary services and resources internally, encouraging and enabling the development of its own employees; and to develop training programmes and materials for external members of the company's extended enterprise, primarily suppliers and Rover dealers. Total quality – 'Hearts and Minds' is a typical example of how RLB in conjunction with Rover Purchasing, created a tailored, specific learning package for suppliers. Rover Employee-Assisted Learning (REAL) was also introduced to encourage self-development by providing financial assistance for a broad range of learning programmes.

To enable 'Agents of Change' to operate cohesively within Rover's own business and to work within their supplier strategies, investment in training in addition to internal coaching become an integral part of the business strategy. This resulted in integrated manufacturing learning programmes inside a structured and progressive development training ladder, enhancing the skills of the majority of the company's purchasing population. Rover Purchasing received the Investors In People (IIP) Award in May 1994 in recognition of the commitment to developing and involving its people. This was also considered an important element in enabling suppliers to raise performance.

Many small- to medium-sized companies have not yet recognized the strategic significance of the purchasing role and, as such, purchasing resources do not exist to develop and integrate their own supply chain within their businesses. This attitude must change if improvement and excellence are to be fully realized.

Supplier development teams (SDTs) will be a key driver in future relationships with suppliers. Although these are operating at present through the best practice techniques and RG 2000, with convergence towards an optimized supply base through supplier reduction, dedicated teams combining these activities will form a seamless group. Multifunctional in formation, Rover's vision embraces the business at large in working with key suppliers who are fully enrolled in its plans. The SDT approach provides the vital link in this vision.

Business effectiveness measures converted into specific action plans will also form the basis for ongoing performance improvement at each supplier and equally within Rover. This forms the thrust of the 'Rover Tomorrow Four' programme. BEMs are the platform designed to close the gap towards world-class benchmarked standards. Rover products introduced in the last five years demonstrate PPM values of no greater than 200 in internal processes. However, delivered quality PPMs are still far in excess of 'world-class' levels in the UK and this is being addressed by individual PPM improvement planning at component level with suppliers to control variation.

Project management processes, by which Rover simultaneously engineers new vehicle products together with suppliers, will also benefit from further process refinements and greater concentration toward increased effectiveness. The correctness of the product design from concept stage, predetermines hours per car to manufacture and build, quality and reliability and not least cost/price relationship (as well as manning levels). Newly developed project management criteria will be added to the company's processes to ensure best practice is applied at the front end of design activity, particularly in the areas of supplier process capability and facility/equipment effectiveness.

In conclusion, Rover has progressively introduced culture change in the drive for continuous improvement to become a 'world-class' company. This culture has been reflected externally in the relationship with its supplier base. Making partnership work is a challenge it believes it has begun to achieve with success, but the journey towards 'world class' must continue by sharing goals, values and greater understanding of each other's businesses. Full supply chain integration beyond the strategic (first-tier) suppliers, and working together to close the gap to the vision of a world competitive supplier base, are goals the company will consistently pursue in its quest for excellence.

Further reading

Anderson Consulting (1993), 'The Lean Enterprise Benchmark Project,' Anderson Consulting, London.

Imai M. (1986), *Kaizen: the Key to Japan's competitive success*, Random House, New York.

Kearney, A.T. (1992), *Total Quality: Time to take off the rose-tinted spectacles*, IFS, Kempston.

Rover Group (1991), 'Supplier Business Specification RG 2000,' Rover Group Purchasing, Birmingham.

4 The automotive industry – the supplier's perspective: a study of Tallent Engineering

Clive Wheeler,
Operations Director, Tallent Engineering

Tallent Engineering Ltd (TEL) is a supplier of complex high-volume chassis structural components to the automotive industry on a just-in-time (JIT) basis. It has grown from a £2m subcontractor in the early 1980s, with little business focus, to a strategic supplier of component parts to 12 car plants throughout Europe with an annual sales turnover of £90m. Following a management buyout in the late 1980s, the company was acquired by the Thyssen Group in the early 1990s. This has enabled it to be positioned as an important supplier in an increasingly global components market.

The success of the company has, in no small measure, been due to the partnerships developed with its customers. To make partnerships work a restructuring process has been undertaken by TEL to focus on the performance which is demanded by its customers. The chapter examines the partnership experience of TEL and highlights the main issues for its effective operation. The account of the company's experience of partnership is not from a solely commercial perspective, but illustrates the fundamental changes necessary to make partnerships successful.

Pressures for change

Competitive pressures to reduce cost with an over-capacity in the automotive sector have stimulated a need for lean organization practices throughout the supply chain, in the areas of design, cost, quality and delivery; this has resulted in intense competition in the components supply industry. Lamming (1993) and Hines (1994) have predicted a 40 per cent reduction in numbers employed in the automotive components supply industry by the end of the decade.

Other effects of the pressure on car manufacturers to reduce cost and improve productivity include a greater responsibility for design resting with the supplier and a trend towards the supplier providing higher-level assemblies, resulting in both great structural changes and a redefinition of responsibilities. The Ford Motor Company, in particular, is looking for suppliers to take more design responsibility and to relocate satellite module assembly plants close to its car assembly plants. These structural changes are proposed against a background of supplier relationships and trust. In addition, Ford's globalization plans have raised the stakes still higher, accelerating structural changes throughout the components industry.

Conflict versus co-operation

What does the term partnership mean? What are the characteristics of one supplier who operates within a 'partnership' régime as compared to that which operates in a more 'traditional' environment? The differences in approach are illustrated in Figure 4.1.

The inefficiencies and overlaps caused by the traditional approach are self-evident: designs which are difficult to produce, high costs, insecurity leading to a lack of willingness to invest, and high defect levels with poor root cause investigation.

It can be argued that at the heart of the differences between traditional and partnership arrangements as shown in Figure 4.1 is a lack of trust in traditional relationships. The main bar-

	Traditional	Best practice		Partnership
Involvement in design	Build to print	Design review	Integral to design process	Turnkey to performance specification
Cost Information	Detail	Grey box		Black box
Cost responsibility	Price only	Customer request	Detailed cost understanding	Shared cost responsibility
Supplier relationship	Purchase order adversarial	Blanket controls still adversarial	Customized collaboration partnership	
Order duration	1 year	3–5 years	Lifetime	
Quality process	Incoming materials inspected	Self-inspect	Process certification	On-site process engineer Engineer exchange
Supply chain integration	Purchase order drivers	MRP drivers	JIT	Fully synchronized

Figure 4.1   Conflict to co-operation: summary of trends

rier to progress towards ever leaner supply chains in the auto-motive components supply industry is the result of years of broken promises, abuses of confidence and general acrimony. Some progress has been made in a small number of firms. In developing new working arrangements with their suppliers, most vehicle manufacturers still appear to deal more in rhetoric than reality. Clearly this is a situation which cannot continue if car producers and suppliers are to achieve 'world-class' performance.

Tallent is a relative newcomer to automotive components supply and has flourished by achieving good working relation-ships with its customers. However, its performance has not always been exemplary. In the latter part of the 1980s the com-pany went through a period of significant growth, coincident with the highest level of recorded sales of European vehicles in history. The growing pains in the company resulted in prob-lems in both delivery and quality performance, along with other suppliers. In 'world-class' terms the company was signif-icantly lacking; a gap that has been closed in recent years. The customers of TEL saw its potential and were impressed by the commitment of the senior management team to improvement. They knew the company would get it right and stayed loyal. To quote Peter Hill, the Purchasing Director of Nissan Motor Manufacturing (UK) Ltd:

Nissan sticks with suppliers when times are tough. When the Primera was launched in 1990, some suppliers were struggling to cope and there were internal pressures to get rid of them. However, we built on the experience and together corrected mis-takes. Two years later, those same suppliers came in with a near perfect launch of the Micra.

Tallent Engineering Ltd was one of those suppliers.

As far as the automotive manufacturers are concerned, a con-siderable variety of cultures has built up within their respective companies. Senior managers in each, however, have one thing in common – they are wedded to the concept of partnership, even if their interpretation varies. In order to achieve it, a variety of strategies of implementation are deployed.

Working with customers

A DTI/SMMT (1994) report indicated that UK component suppliers were the 'worst in Europe', making the point that no UK suppliers were 'world class'.

The author of this chapter recently completed a two-week tour of Japan and the USA, studying the benchmarks for the specific sector of the industry in which TEL operates. One conclusion is that the best performing companies have developed robust partnerships with individual customers over many decades. Stability, growth and mutual reliance, leading to trust in the relationship, has resulted in confident operation and profitable performance. The conditions have consequently been created to allow the necessary strategic investments in state-of-the-art equipment. Perhaps more fundamentally, although not surprisingly, there is substantial evidence of strong alignment of suppliers in a single-customer relationship throughout their organizations. This applies broadly across the range of company activities from strategy to shopfloor visual management techniques. As well as this alignment characteristic, the single-customer base allows integration of systems including commercial, financial, quality, production control and design.

In general, the European supply base is not structured in this way and each component supplier serves many customers. Each vehicle manufacturer has its own quality management system, production control system, design system and order system which is perceived by each as a source of competitive advantage. Duplication of all these different systems to achieve the same end leads to one of the main reasons for the Japan/Europe productivity gap.

How then is it possible to gain the interface and alignment advantages of a single-customer business in a multiple-customer organization? At TEL the organization has been restructured into customer-related groups with a resulting improvement in customer service, focus and accountability. The company's main customers are Ford, Nissan, Rover and Honda. There are now teams in place who are dedicated to servicing their own customers, thus achieving the benefits of Japanese best practice with the attributes of the Western approach.

Each of TEL's customers has a slightly different approach to its suppliers, the main characteristics of which are now examined.

The Ford Motor Company has recently undergone important restructuring to integrate its purchasing and engineering activities within its global product development policy. With a focus on supply chain cost reduction, supplier–customer teams have been established to search out opportunities for savings under a programme called 'Drive for leadership'. The savings achieved were shared with suppliers to bring about a reduction in cost. These initiatives continue and now include a quality operating system (QOS), which is a tool for supporting improvement, and the QS 9000 system. One of the strengths of the Ford Motor Company is its ability to offer to the supply base very professionally designed tools and techniques for control and improvement (e.g. it was one of the first companies to request that suppliers provide evidence of process capability through the use of statistical process control (SPC)), and it continues to offer the best packages and advice on the subject. Its strategic emphasis, in relation to the supplier base, is now focused on the development of product and components to meet world demand, manifested in the global sourcing policies within the 'Ford 2000' programme.

Nissan Motor Manufacturing (UK) Ltd takes a very strategic view of its approach to suppliers and their development. The company operates a well organized objective measurement system of supplier performance and feeds back results in five categories: quality, cost, delivery, development and management (QCDDM). In common with other Japanese vehicle manufacturers it has had a strong influence over the development of the UK components supply industry, the result of which has been a considerable improvement in performance across all aspects of the business. Exceptional improvement and performance is recognized annually in a supplier awards ceremony. The continuous improvement of the best suppliers to Nissan makes meeting the requisite performance criteria more difficult to achieve each year. The focus is on continuous and company-wide improvement. Support for suppliers is achieved through a dedicated supplier development team, local supplier group meetings and visits to Nissan suppliers in Japan. Operationally there is assistance with improvement activities, including set-up time reduction and workshop management implementation (Genba Kanri). At the strategic level Nissan enlisted the support of UMIST in a programme known as 'Strategy for Success'. Tallent participated in this programme in the early 1990s, achieving further clarity of 'mission' as a result. Much of the improvement at Tallent has been assisted by the close relationships it has developed with Nissan.

Rover also developed a strategic approach to supplier performance improvement. The programme was known as 'RG 2000' which included a business survey development carried out in conjunction with the University of Warwick. This survey measured improvements in all aspects of the business. Rover was also aiming to achieve major improvements in customer satisfaction through improved delivery of vehicles. The objective was to achieve a two-week delivery of cars ordered. The supplier development team at Rover focused on logistics improvement and measured objectives included:

- less than 100 parts per million (PPM) delivered defects
- 100 per cent on-time delivery and correct quantity
- flexibility and proactivity
- direct interface to Electronics Data Interchange (EDI) from suppliers' planning systems with no intervention and used to communicate with sub-suppliers using Odette standards
- part lead time of 0 to 1 day.

By working closely with Rover and having related overall business measures, TEL now meets all these requirements.

Taking the initiative with customers

Whilst the approaches clearly differ between car companies, overall objectives are similar, i.e. to achieve 'world-class' suppliers. Some of the measures which determine 'world-class' performance have been established and verified, facilitated by the relationship TEL has in Japan with suppliers to Nissan. Clear and measurable goals need to be present in the organization to close the gap and achieve 'world-class' performance. Nissan established such goals with NX96 (Nissan Excellence NX96 in 1996). TEL responded by evaluating this initiative for its entire organization and established TX96 (Tallent Excellence in 1996).

Since 1992 considerable improvements in key performance indicators have been achieved at TEL:

Performance indicators	End 1992	End 1994	End 1996
Delivered quality PPM	600	50	25
Die change time (minutes)	240	30	10
Days of inventory days	20	10	5
Delivery performance %	90	100	100
Cost reduction index	100	90	80
Design capability % (based on grey box design capability)	20	70	100

How have these measures been established?

Realizing that the Japanese supply chain provides the minimum cost, UK suppliers to Nissan visited its Japanese suppliers in Japan to examine the concepts working in practice. They were then expected to implement the best practice techniques, systems and practices 'back home'. Some examples of where suppliers were proactive with customers included:

Cost
- regular meetings with customers to examine the total cost of acquisition
- value analysis techniques
- Kaizen teams

Design
- cross-functional teams
- offering the customer alternative solutions

procurement/TQM
packaging

Delivery
- means of delivery – e.g. returnable packaging designed by supplier
- EDI – delivery information.

What does the European automotive industry want from its suppliers?

First and foremost it wants supplies to be sourced from organizations who achieve best practice, leading to lowest cost procurement. Within the European component supply base this does not normally apply, and rapid improvement is essential. Suppliers must be aware of their own performance in all activities and how it compares with the best in the world, and then commit themselves to a self-sustaining process of closing the gap.

Unfortunately this does not always prevail in Western Europe, where a considerable degree of mistrust between supplier and customer still exists.

To satisfy the demands of its customer, the automotive component supplier must commit an increasing amount of resources to design and development. At the same time, there is an increasing expectation of productivity and ever-growing delegation of responsibility. For some suppliers this has important implications for product liability and there are examples where the insurance premium to protect against potential claims have doubled the cost of the piece part prices. A presence at the earliest stage of development is now expected from the supplier. Indeed, with integrated European/worldwide purchasing responsibilities, it is often necessary to open sales offices close to or even within the customer's engineering departments.

work-in teams

In short, it is an increasingly demanding market where suppliers are expected to perform by anticipating the customer's every need. The rewards are ever-higher barriers to entry and long-term relationships.

Changing attitudes, structures and practices

All the automotive vehicle manufacturers are demanding higher levels of customer service. They have entered an era where quality and delivery have ceased to be differentiators, instead they have become prerequisites or qualifiers. The differentiators are now flexibility, design capability in the way of offering solutions to the customer and a focus on cost reduction. An ability to manage the supply chain is also sought. Consequently a great shift in attitude is taking place. Everyone in the industry must recognize the impact of factors such as globalization, long-term contracts, total supply chain management, cost reduction, reduction in the number of suppliers and the requirement to maximize added value to the product. Changes were made to the organization structure of TEL to respond to these demands from its customers.

A revised organization was established in the early 1990s. Customer-focused teams were formed in the commercial and operations functions, led by product group managers with a broad portfolio of responsibility. The long-term intention was to develop these managers into 'mini-general managers'. The revised structure has been successful and has resulted in improvements in:

- involvement
- focus and ownership of customer/product
- focus on method improvement and quality
- teamwork on new product introduction
- shared customer vision
- alignment of people and systems
- clearly defined responsibility and accountability.

Each product group contains personnel from maintenance, production control, product development, quality and industrial engineering (renamed improvement support), supported by finance, purchasing, IT and sales staff.

To avoid duplication and a proliferation of different systems the managers of the original support functions remain with a small support staff. However, their job has changed from a line responsibility to one of ensuring best practice, providing training, interchanging ideas and managing the infrastructure.

Fewer people are involved and matrix responsibility is now in operation. The revised structure has been particularly successful in improving teamwork on new product introduction. With customer alignment each member of the team feels a sense of ownership of, and responsibility for, new products under a separate project leader.

Going down the supply chain

In the first-tier supplier base a continuous improvement philosophy has developed from direct contact with vehicle manufacturers. The extent of understanding of the need for commitment to continuous improvement in the sub-suppliers (second and third tier) is variable. Some of these sub-suppliers are themselves direct suppliers to vehicle manufacturers, but there is an issue of awareness and implementation. In order to overcome these shortfalls, TEL still has in place a programme of supplier development. The company has about 60 suppliers of production components which are usually single-sourced. For supplier partnerships to work effectively, similar improvement philosophies must be adopted by TEL's suppliers. Sometimes this is preaching to the converted but, frequently, sub-suppliers do not have an effective improvement process in place and neither appreciate nor achieve 'world-class' levels of quality, cost and delivery. For example, incoming PPM levels to TEL have historically been 500 and deliveries are rarely precise. The situation is improving with senior management, even in the larger suppliers, recognizing that customer demands are consistent with their own business aspirations.

Tallent has its own quality management system survey and inspection of incoming parts has been virtually eliminated. Supplier quality assurance (SQA) has been replaced by supplier quality improvement (SQI) and purchasing has a strategic role concerned with supplier-base improvement and new vendor selection and appraisal for new products. As for the relationships which TEL has established with automotive manufacturers, the production control departments of suppliers interface directly with the company and quality issues are dealt with, operationally at least, within the internal product groups. (There are few shared component parts.)

The vendor assessment system ensures the information is collated and the purchasing department monitors and feeds back performance data to suppliers.

What was formerly TEL's industrial engineering department is now focused on improvement support and much of its work is directed towards the supplier base. In particular, some less developed suppliers benefit from implementing the techniques which TEL has learned, sometimes from customers.

To establish a common understanding amongst all suppliers, a conference was organized explaining the company's TX strategies and outlining the important part which suppliers have to play.

The next phase of development will be to push these concepts further back in the supply chain to third or even fourth-tier suppliers. Based on the experience of TEL, it is clear that the further back in the supply chain one goes, the less awareness exists amongst suppliers of the need to pursue 'world-class' levels of performance. A notable exception to this is British Steel, which in recent years has progressed greatly in customer partnerships.

Benefits and lessons learnt

The positive influence that the Japanese car companies have had on the improvement of the European components industry is hard to overstate, particularly in the UK. Measures of performance show how far the industry has come, even if it still has a long way to go to compete with world best. Partnership in the automotive sector has resulted in a number of distinct benefits including:

- stability of business
- strategic partnerships in the component sector
- early supplier selection and subsequent design for manufacture
- effective cost management
- improvement culture
- confidence for investment
- confidence in the future without complacency.

An additional benefit will accrue during the late 1990s. It is predicted that by this time 100,000 jobs will be lost from the UK component industry. Within a growth market and resulting supplier-base reduction it follows that there will be winners and losers. Partnership arrangements under these circumstances help to ensure a component supplier survives and prospers over this period of change.

Not all the benefits are one-sided. There are great advantages in partnership for the customer, including:

- reduced lead times
- reduced inventory
- competitive prices and costs
- improved quality
- consistent delivery (given stable schedules)
- high-level modular assembly.

In addition, the OEM benefits from an increasing design and development capability from the supplier. This leads to shorter timescales for new product introduction, improved quality on commencement of production and reduced cost. Also there is progression towards less liability for warranty costs and reduced product liability risk for the vehicle manufacturers.

A key area of effective sourcing is early supplier involvement in the new product development process. It is important to both the supplier and customer, as product development increasingly plays a more important part in future business development. The main issue is that the lessons learned from prototype manufacture are incorporated into process development. Globalization is increasing opportunities and threats in such a process.

In summary, partnership has become a way of life for Tallent Engineering. It is not a cosy existence but a way of doing business through teamwork which matches internal company philosophies. It is a means whereby both partners can achieve the benefits of working together to achieve end-user specification through a process of constant improvement in a market where increasingly 'good enough' is just not 'good enough'!

Footnote, November 1997

Since this chapter was written the situation has moved on apace. When Ford's Chairman, Alex Trotman, introduced the 'Ford 2000' to reorganize the company, he predicted a brutal world: too many car makers, over capacity and insufficient profit. His mistake was not in forecasting that it would happen, but when – it's happening now. Indeed, competition has intensified at a rate never envisaged five years ago.

Amongst the implications for suppliers is that purchasing is no longer a regional function for Ford – it's a global enterprise. Ford is putting suppliers into developing markets more quickly through a programme called 'follow sourcing'. To quote some suppliers: 'Follow sourcing is forcing us to test our faith in Ford's good intentions'. Others, meanwhile, complain: 'It is an inflexible practice that is eroding supplier margins by forcing them to build excess capacity'. The truth is that it is the price of doing business in these market conditions. Tallent Engineering has been involved in 'follow sourcing' commitments in a big way.

In March 1997 Budd and Tallent (both divisions of Thyssen) announced the building of a new plant at Hopkinsville, Kentucky, to serve local OEM customers – initially primarily Ford. Other joint ventures to support the customer around the world are currently under consideration. Whilst Thyssen Budd Automotive Division has been formed from a collection of previously largely separate business units, Tower, a US stamping company, has acquired A. O. Smith, another stamping company. Thyssen and Krupp Hoesch recently announced a proposal to merge, with major synergies envisaged in the automotive sector. These are examples of an increasing trend towards mergers, acquisitions and rationalizations.

Meanwhile, full-service status has been achieved at TEL. Development of other customer business continues and full use is being made of recently expanded design and development facilities.

As this footnote is being written, the NX96 programme of Nissan draws to a close, to be replaced by NEXT 21 (Nissan European Excellence Towards 21st Century). There is only a brief pause to reflect on the supplier achievements of NX96 (including 85 to 97.4 per cent on time delivery and 1150 PPM quality in 1992 to less than 100 PPM in 1996), before considering the challenges of NEXT 21 which include:

- shorter development lead times
- intensifying quality demands
- reduced number of vehicle trials
- increased vehicle launch rate
- dramatic cost reduction.

Here too, the key to the success of NEXT 21 will be a globally competitive supply chain.

Honda continues with a most demanding régime of QCD with exacting measures. Its catchphrase for suppliers is: 'We only want good parts'. They mean it!

Throughout the entire OEM customer base, cost has become a highly focused issue, with all OEMs demanding and receiving price/cost reductions over the last twelve months. Clearly for UK suppliers like Tallent, the recent strength of the pound is a threat to global competitiveness and further increases pressure to become 'quality driven and waste free'. The nature of the pressures on suppliers is illustrated in Figure 4.2.

In the early 1990s it was predicted that by the end of the century quality and delivery would become prerequisites with design, cost and ability to manage supplier base as differentiators. This has come true early. The implications for supplier/customer relationships have in some respects been to polarize adversarial and partnership approaches.

The market has become tougher. Those who are surviving (survival being a *continuous* requirement) will exploit ever-increasing opportunities – the rest will simply disappear.

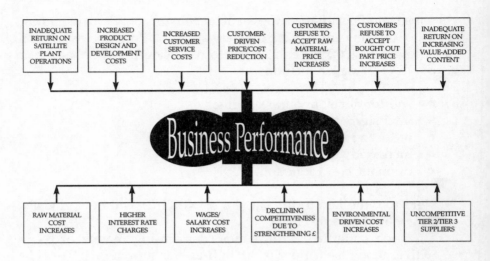

Figure 4.2   The cost squeeze

Further reading

Andersen Consulting, (1993), The Lean Enterprise Benchmark Project: Report, Andersen Consulting, London.

DTI/SMMT, (1991), Supplier Innovation: 'Opportunities for small and medium U.K. automotive components companies', Department of Trade and Industry, London.

DTI/SMMT, (1994), 'A review of the relationship between vehicle manufacturers and suppliers', Department of Trade and Industry, London.

Hines P., (1994), *Creating World Class Suppliers: Unlocking Mutual Competitive Advantage*, Pitman, London.

Kearney A. T., (1992), *Total Quality: Time to Take off the Rose-Tinted Spectacles*, IFS: Kempston.

Lamming R., (1993), *Beyond Partnership: Strategies for Innovation and Lean Supply*, Prentice-Hall, Hemel Hempstead.

5 Supplier partnerships: a study of Cosalt Holiday Homes

Mike J Isaac,
Cosalt Holiday Homes

Cosalt Holiday Homes is a medium-sized enterprise that manufactures holiday homes and is part of Cosalt Plc whose headquarters is in Grimsby. The main activities of Cosalt Plc are caravan manufacture, ships' chandlery, fibre manufacturers, workwear, finance and commercial lighting. The annual sales turnover of group activities in 1995 was £86m.

This chapter examines Cosalt Holiday Homes' process of improvement, starting with the introduction of quality control circles through to its supplier partnership initiative. The rationale behind developing the supplier base and its supplier partnership strategy will be examined and the key stages involved in the process will be highlighted, together with the achievements, benefits and failures.

Cosalt's quality programme

In the 1980s Cosalt Holiday Homes set itself a target to become a world-class manufacturing organization (as defined by Lascelles and Dale, 1991). To help to achieve this the directors introduced a quality management approach to the business. Quality became the main business driver and this was started with the introduction of quality control circles (QCCs) – groups of employees who meet periodically to:

- pinpoint, examine, analyse and solve problems, looking not only at quality issues, but also handling, productivity, cost, safety and a range of work-related issues
- enhance the communication between employees and management.

A QCC usually comprises eight to twelve employees where the membership is voluntary and whose activities are guided by a facilitator (see Dale, 1994). Quality circles were introduced in 1987 and thrived, and led the company to find out what other tools, techniques, systems and initiatives were available and applicable to Cosalt's operating environment.

A visit to Japan and to some of its successful manufacturing companies was made in 1989 by the author. The purpose of the visit was to learn about successful improvement strategies. The concept of Kaizen was considered to be particularly useful (see Imai, 1986) and was subsequently implemented at Cosalt.

Kaizen essentially means continuous improvement; seeking small improvements through the elimination of waste. These activities complement QCCs and together have proved to be very successful at Cosalt. A vision of a total quality approach began to emerge from the Kaizen concept. This led to the investigation of a much broader approach using the BS 5750 series of quality management system standards (now known as BS EN ISO 9000) as the base.

The decision to aim for BS 5750: Part 2 (now BS EN ISO 9002) registration was questioned by some of Cosalt's directors, with a number doubting its value. One concern was that Cosalt's clients lacked an appreciation of the value of BS 5750: Part 2 requirements. Another problem was more disconcerting. Some of Cosalt's suppliers who had achieved such registration had often supplied materials and components containing defects, thus raising doubts about the standard's effectiveness. On balance, however, the board of directors felt that the standard was common sense and that it should not be blamed for the inadequate implementation of its clauses. Subsequently the requirements of BS 5750: Part 2 were implemented and registration achieved. Further QCCs and Kaizen were harnessed and developed into a company-wide approach to quality management. However, internal quality improvements highlighted the need for suppliers to improve their performance. This focus on supplier partnership in Cosalt's total quality approach was necessary given its own business context.

Cosalt Holiday Homes is an assembly-type factory where limited manufacturing is performed, but the final product is assembled from a large number of externally sourced components. The real skill base of Cosalt's workforce lies in its ability to assemble components and in cutting accurately the various timber-based materials. Success in achieving a final product of the requisite quality therefore depends to a large extent on competitively priced supplies which conform to requirements. This is essential because 70 per cent of the selling price of holiday homes is attributable to purchased components. Cosalt thus focused attention on its supplier base, whilst maintaining and improving the internal initiatives already in place.

The rationale behind supplier partnership

The main aim of developing the supplier base was to secure a competitive edge in terms of quality, design input and cost structure. Cosalt turned to supplier partnership to build in a guarantee of stability of costs for a minimum of six or, ideally, twelve months, and also to see improvements in each of the other two key areas. This was important because of the dependence that Cosalt had on its suppliers for quality, and hence business viability. It was also important in the face of a dynamic and highly competitive business environment.

The grounding of a supplier partnership strategy

Bevan (1989) argues that the management of change with respect to supplier development falls into two main areas:

- Changing attitudes and gaining commitment from suppliers, staff and other people in the company who must be persuaded to adopt a new approach in their dealings with each other.
- Changing procedures and practices which are historical (i.e. communication and control procedures like scheduling, source selection and contract terms and conditions).

Building on this, the key features of supplier partnership, especially in relation to attitudes and procedures, have been outlined by Lascelles and Dale (1989):

1 Establish and articulate programme objectives.
2 Set priorities for action.
3 Identify key suppliers as potential long-term partners and make plans to reduce supplier base.
4 Assess the capability of suppliers to meet purchase requirements.
5 Engage in advanced quality planning with suppliers.
6 Formally recognize suppliers which achieve preferred status.
7 Develop an ongoing quality improvement relationship with suppliers based on a free exchange of information.

The work, of Bevan (1989) and Lascelles and Dale (1989) provided the framework for the supplier partnership programme launched by Cosalt. Having operated a supplier partnership for some years, Cosalt have refined it and, in particular, tailored it to the needs of small- and medium-sized companies.

Methodology for small- and medium-sized enterprises (SMEs)

Based on Cosalt's experience of supplier partnership, a six-stage methodology has been developed (see Figure 5.1). These six stages will now be discussed in detail.

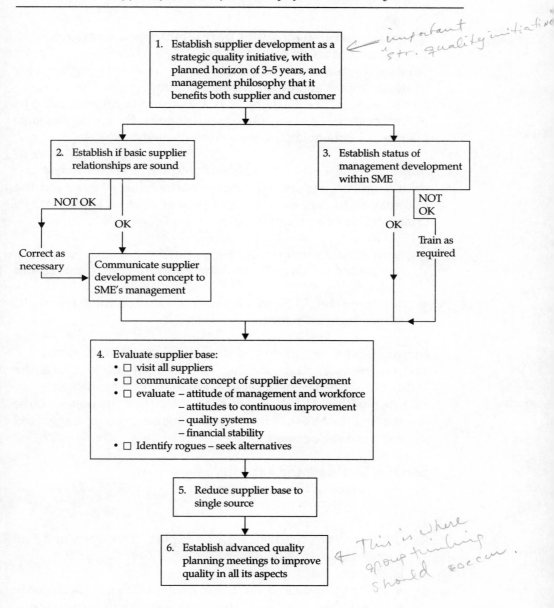

Figure 5.1   Flow diagram for SMEs embarking upon supplier development

suggestive
length
of
agreement

Stage 1: Establish supplier partnership as a strategic improvement initiative

Supplier partnership should be viewed as a three to five year strategic improvement initiative, including in its mission statement that supplier partnership is a philosophy offering benefits to both customer and supplier. Following this the concept of supplier development should be communicated to key staff.

Stage 2: Establish status of basic supplier relationship

Prior to embarking upon a supplier partnership programme, the two diagnostic criteria outlined below should be considered to establish if the company is ready for partnerships:

- Lead times, delivery schedules, payment terms and conditions must be agreed and adhered to by both supplier and customer.
- Suppliers should be treated with the respect they deserve as fellow business partners.

Stage 3: Establish status of management development

The company should examine its management to assess the status of its development. The lesson learned from research carried out within Cosalt (Isaac, 1995) was that managers must understand the basics of management before becoming involved in strategic development.

Stage 4: Evaluate the supplier base

The main steps of the evaluation are:

1   Visit all suppliers.
2   Communicate the concept of supplier development to all suppliers.
3   Evaluate:
    - attitudes and values of the management and workforce
    - attitudes to quality assurance and quality improvement
    - the health of the quality management system
    - financial stability.
4   Identify rogue suppliers and seek alternatives.

Stage 5: Reduce the supplier base to single source

It is recommended that a task force is established which should be multidisciplined, have known negotiation skills and be led by a director as team leader. The task force should evaluate the supplier base using a strengths, weaknesses, opportunities and threats (SWOT) analysis. In this stage emphasis is placed on replacing rogue suppliers. The characteristics of these suppliers are arrogance, complacency and a belief that price increases are a right and should not be negotiated. Their quality of supplies tends to be indifferent and they are usually in a monopoly supply situation. The time involved to eliminate or convert rogue suppliers is considerable and communication is vital. For example, at Cosalt it took 70 per cent of three senior personnel's time for one year.

Stage 6: Establish advanced quality planning meetings

The research of Isaac (1995) has shown that this stage is the lifeblood of the supplier partnership. It is highly recommended that advanced quality planning meetings should be held on a regular basis. An agenda similar to the one used at Cosalt to form the framework for this vital stage should be considered (see Figure 5.2). The research has also shown that for this stage to be successful flat structures facilitate communications and they are vastly improved simply by holding these meetings on a regular basis. Empowerment is also necessary to allow the operational managers of both customer and supplier to communicate effectively with each other. Note that Stages 4, 5 and 6 are iterative.

Other salient features of this stage include broader participation, more consensus decision making and showing greater respect and concern for people employed in both the customer's organization as well as the supplier's. It is also recommended that rating assessments are used in the supplier development meetings to monitor delivery performance.

Strategic supplier partnership versus short-term

Based on the Cosalt experience it is strongly recommended that supplier partnership is considered as a strategic quality manage-

1. Quality
   1.1   Product quality
   1.2   Information
   1.3   Communication
   1.4   Service
         - delivery
         - quotations
         - specifications, costings and terms

2. Lead times (reduction and maintenance of)

3. Stock levels (reduction, maintenance and cost of)

4. Aftersales
   4.1   Service
   4.2   Lead times
   4.3   Availability of materials

5. Product development
   5.1   Constant improvement
   5.2   Optimization
   5.3   Prototypes (supplier involvement)

6. Any other business

Figure 5.2   Supplier development meeting agenda

ment initiative. It is recognized, however, that there might be situations where the term of three to five years may not be practicable. Hence, the issue of strategic supplier partnership will be considered versus the short-term situation.

Lopez postulates that short-term situations cannot afford to be ignored (Syson (1994)). Whilst working for Volkswagen he confronted suppliers in an adversarial manner demanding considerable reductions in the cost of purchased components, or alternative suppliers would be given the work. Lopez would appear to be justifying his action in times of recession, arguing that everyone involved in automobile manufacture should share the burden when necessary. He effectively reintroduced short-term price opportunities back on the agenda in a somewhat adversarial way. It is clear that business needs to adopt this approach in times of recession and so the recommended methodology will remind SMEs, who are considering supplier development, that this is an issue which they may have to consider.

A key question in the long-term versus short-term approach to supplier partnership is: 'How closely can the principles of supplier partnership be met if (a) only one year is available, or (b) only two years are available?'.

If only *one year is available* then the main steps involved are:

- Hold internal communication meetings to introduce the concept of supplier development to management and staff.
- Decide which are the three most important suppliers to the company.
- Invite the top three suppliers' board members to the SME's premises to introduce and explain the supplier development concepts.
- Arrange site visits to the top three suppliers' premises to introduce and explain supplier partnership to the suppliers' management and staff.
- Set up advanced quality planning meetings. Research and practical experience at Cosalt has shown that these meetings are vital to supplier partnerships and are the vehicle for having an impact on quality, communication, lead time reduction etc. It is suggested that these meetings are held <u>monthly</u>.

If only *two years are available* then it is recommended that the stages involved for one year duration are followed, but in this case select the six most important suppliers to the business. Again the setting up of the advanced quality planning meetings is of paramount importance but for the second year the meetings may not need to be held at more than 2–3 month intervals.

When supplier partnership is underway consider a monitoring system to improve and develop the strategy by highlighting the areas that require further work. A checklist that is in effect an operational validation of the principles of supplier development may be useful. The one given in Figure 5.3 helps to improve the

Supplier development principle	Characteristic	
1 Holistic	Scope deployed	0–25%
		25–50%
		50–75%
		75–100%
2 Empowerment	• clearly defined responsibilities	
	• clearly mapped and measured processes	
	• discretionary action	
	• joint initiatives/processes	
3 Communication	• clear points of communication	
	• scope of communication	
	• methods (e mail, EDI)	
4 Continuous improvement	• basic tools	
	• quality systems	
	• policy deployment	
	• process improvement	
	• benchmarking	
	• self-assessment	
5 Mutual benefit	• clear quantified benefits	
	• 'open-book' approach	
	• target costing	
	• mutual help group (networking and benchmarking)	
6 Attitude	• adversarial	
	• co-operative	
	• partnering	
	• comakership	
7 Negotiation	• joint	
	• scope of agreement (warranties, terms of payment)	
	• confidentiality	
	• procedures for settling disputes	
8 Good management	• organization design	
	• management development (training, Investors in People, benchmarking, job rotation)	
	• empowerment	
	• attitude surveys	
9 Long-term business partnerships	• strategic suppliers (added-value business relationships)	
	• mutual economic benefit	
	• establish joint technological advantage	
	• strong joint customer/market perception	

Figure 5.3   Checklist for evaluating supplier development performance

Ok, they've got checklist for evaluating supplier dev, but what about evaluation of quality groups in the partnership?

supplier partnership strategy by highlighting those areas that require further work. It shows the principles and the corresponding operational characteristics. A company evaluating the progress of its supplier partnership programme can decide which characteristics have already been met and hence what others may be considered to improve their strategy.

Findings, achievements and failures

The findings are summarized as follows:

Vmportant!

- Cosalt's non-bureaucratic organization and flat structure helped communications, especially when dealing with similarly structured suppliers. The same good management principles should be applied to the supplier base as to the internal organization. Standards must be set and maintained. Credibility, respect, trust and involvement will pay dividends and the stability of longer-term contracts will give confidence to suppliers and enhance loyalty. Empowerment was necessary to allow the operational managers of both Cosalt Holiday Homes and its suppliers to become effective. The creation of a blame-free environment was sought to facilitate continuous improvement and to encourage a win–win situation.
- With some rogue companies only the surprise of competition forced a response. Competitive prices became a very important feature of Stage 1 of the supplier development model. The arrogance and complacency among some suppliers was broken down by nurturing alternatives, with the original supplier having to win back the lost business. Cosalt's window and door supplier is a good example of this. The alternative supplier now has 100 per cent of Cosalt's business.
- The supplier base is vital to a manufacturing company like Cosalt; considerable time must be devoted to this area on an on-going basis. In the past a lack of attention was clearly detrimental to Cosalt's business performance.
- Cosalt was charged too much for its components prior to the supplier development initiative. It is likely that many other SMEs are suffering in the same way.

- There is a wealth of experience and expertise among the supplier base that must not be ignored.
- Without exception suppliers were very enthusiastic about partnership and wanted to take a very active part, even some of the rogue suppliers.
- Very few suppliers had embarked upon supplier partnership and even these had made no great progress to date.
- There is a growing awareness of the importance of quality, after-sales service, customer satisfaction, reduction in stock, JIT and lead-time reduction. The wind of change has started to blow, at least through Cosalt's suppliers.
- The general view of Cosalt, seen through the eyes of the supplier base, is that it is a very progressive, stable company.
- In some cases Cosalt's purchasing power had a very limited effect on the size of some suppliers' annual turnover – a point made to Cosalt whenever this occurred. One company mentioned that they could achieve Cosalt's annual order book in one day.
- Motivation was facilitated by the willingness of suppliers to take part in supplier development.

The main achievements are:

- The principal achievement to date must be the financial savings. These are in the order of 5 per cent of cost and for Cosalt that means a saving of some £750K per year. These savings do not take into account the inflationary increases that would have taken place. Experience would suggest a further 3–5 per cent has been saved in this way.
- The realization among suppliers that a way forward to improve their future was on offer and, in their view, one which was based on a common-sense and pragmatic approach.
- Cosalt's management team are very enthusiastic about partnership and their knowledge and expertise is being enhanced. There is also a growing confidence in the task force approach. There is a real sense of involvement and commitment in the company.
- Partnership is involving all strata of management from board

level to first-line management. This level of participation helps to develop a cohesive corporate culture.

There were also failures:

- An early failure was an over eagerness to accept the lowest price on offer. It was all too easy to be seduced by this method, which takes no account of quality. However, with Cosalt's main bought-in components, i.e. ovens and hobs, aluminium and soft furnishings, quality was considered to be more important than cost. Some suppliers attempted 'to buy' business.
- There are still areas within Cosalt where supplier's ideas are not fully encouraged, with some of the attitudes at Cosalt needing to be changed. This flaw must be eradicated if Cosalt is to achieve world-class status.
- Communications from Cosalt to the suppliers are often not good enough. Feedback is essential to optimize this area of business performance, but has proven hard to maintain.
- Gaining exact achievement of specification, quality and lead time is difficult and fraught with problems. Suppliers that are not wholly owned as subsidiaries have conflicting requirements from different customers. A further failure throughout the supplier development programme is the lack of success in convincing the supplier base that it is their responsibility to continually reduce their costs to Cosalt by increasing internal efficiency. When this subject is discussed with the suppliers the reaction tends to be 'we have not increased our prices for say twelve or eighteen months'. This attitude is probably due to the economic situation prevailing during the period of the supplier development initiative.
- Most suppliers are very reluctant for Cosalt to have knowledge of their cost structure. Some suppliers have said that Cosalt should not determine their profitability and that their cost structure should not concern Cosalt.
- In all but two cases, Cosalt suppliers would not continue with supplier partnerships without Cosalt's encouragement.

Summary

The experience at Cosalt has shown that considerable benefits can be obtained by both customers and suppliers when supplier development is practised in an effective manner. It has also shown that supplier partnership is an exciting and potent method for obtaining a competitive edge in terms of cost reductions, quality improvements and design advantages. The advanced quality planning meetings became the life blood of supplier partnership and acted as a vehicle for the considerable improvements which resulted in an increase in market share from 13 to 19 per cent for Cosalt and its suppliers. Communication and empowerment were necessary to create a blame-free environment before the improvements began.

It is recommended that supplier partnership is considered as a strategic quality management initiative. Cosalt's experience of supplier development has also shown that:

- the reduction of the supplier base is crucial
- basic supplier/customer relations must be soundly based prior to commencing supplier partnership.
- management development should allow strategic issues like supplier partnership to be taken on board.

Further reading

Bevan, J. (1989), 'Comakership', *Management Decision*, vol. 27, no. 3, pp. 50–54.

Dale, B.G. (ed) (1994), *Managing Quality* (second edition), Prentice Hall, Herts.

Feigenbaum, A.V. (1982), 'Quality and business growth today', *Quality Progress*, 15 (11), pp. 22–25.

Imai, M. (1986), *Kaizen: the Key to Japan's Competitive Success*, Random House, New York.

Isaac, M. J. (1995), 'Theory and practice of supplier development for small and medium-sized enterprises', Ph.D. thesis, University of Hull.

Lascelles, D.M. and Dale, B.G. (1989), 'The buyer-supplier relationship in total quality management', *Journal of Purchasing and Materials Management*, 25 (2), pp. 10–19.

Lascelles, D.M. and Dale, B.G. (1991), 'Levelling out the future', *The TQM Magazine*, 3 (6), pp. 325–330.

Syson, R. (1994), 'Review of purchasing and supply', proceedings of annual Chartered Institute of Purchasing and Supply conference, June, Mayfair International Hotel, London.

6 Supplier partnerships: assessing the potential and getting started

Bernard Burnes and Paul Whittle

There is considerable interest in supplier partnerships. In the UK, this interest is partly due to government and industrial sponsorship of the concept, including the DTI's Manufacturing into the '90s programme and the joint DTI/CBI sponsorship of Partnership Sourcing Ltd. Perhaps the main impetus however, has come from large customers who have committed themselves to closer and more co-operative relationships with their suppliers. Whilst the initiative was taken up by Japanese transplants such as Nissan Motor Manufacturing (UK) Ltd, there are now a host of other companies who have moved in this direction (e.g. Tesco, Black and Decker, Glaxo and Laing Homes). Nevertheless, the research undertaken at UMIST and elsewhere has shown that many companies still remain to be convinced of the merits and benefits of supplier development (see Burnes and New 1996). 658 · 406 6UR

Having said that, the intention in this chapter is not primarily to convince the sceptical of the benefits of supplier partnerships. Rather it is to show how companies can assess the benefits and drawbacks for themselves. First a word of caution: developing supplier partnerships is a significant, long-term strategic initiative striking at the core of an organisation's competitiveness.

For this reason it is the province of chief executives and senior managers and should be approached with care and deliberation.

Most relationships between customer firms and their suppliers involve a considerable degree of inefficiency and waste. Despite the increasing awareness of good customer–supplier relationships based upon co-operation, many firms find difficulty in setting up such relationships. The reason for this is relatively straightforward. Co-operative supply relationships are not an easy option, as many imagine, but considerably harder to implement than traditional buyer–seller relationships.

(Ian Gibson, Managing Director, Nissan Motor Manufacturing (UK) Ltd)

What is supplier partnership?

Supplier partnership has a variety of definitions, some of which are highly technical and theoretical, whilst others cover the core concepts in a few brief and well-chosen words. The following, by Partnership Sourcing Ltd (1991) captures the spirit of the concept.

[Supplier partnership] is where customer and suppliers develop such a close and long-term relationship that the two work together as partners. It isn't philanthropy: the aim is to secure the best possible commercial advantage. The principle is that teamwork is better than combat. If the end-customer is to be best served, then the parties to a deal must work together – and both must win. [Supplier partnership] works because both parties have an interest in each other's success.

What really defines any concept is its practical requirements. Those companies which are successfully pursuing supplier partnerships all tend to stress that it requires the following conditions:

- a *long-term* commitment
- both customers and suppliers to be *proactive*
- both parties to *integrate* key functions and activities
- a commitment to developing and maintaining *co-operative* and *close relationships*

- a clear and well-structured *framework* for determining cost, price and profit for both sides
- a *win–win* philosophy – both parties must stand to gain from the supplier development approach
- *Continuous improvement* in all spheres of their activities.

Supplier partnership is not a panacea for all known ills. It is an approach to purchasing which recognizes that the competitiveness of most customers is dependent on that of their suppliers. In the majority of companies it is impossible to significantly improve quality or delivery, reduce costs or bring new products to market without a great effort from their suppliers. However, this may not be the case for all companies. Some companies buy in only a small proportion of their final product, others procure mainly raw material which is available on a commodity basis from a number of suppliers and others may be purchasing from a source of limited capacity. For others, yet again, they may be buying from world class suppliers. The situation will vary from company to company. It would be wrong to say in advance that all companies will benefit from supplier partnerships or that all are ready for it. It is up to each company to make its own estimation of the benefits of supplier partnership, and its own decision about whether to proceed with it and, if so, what form supplier development will take in its particular case.

It's up to each company to decide

This chapter now outlines a number of steps which are designed to aid companies in making their own decision. Before proceeding, one point above all others should be stressed: a decision to proceed, or not, with supplier partnership has long-term competitive implications for a business. Such decisions must be taken at the most senior level – they cannot be left solely to individual managers or functional specialists.

A partnering agreement has long term complications for a business

Step 1: Should you consider supplier partnership?

The following questions are designed to allow senior managers to establish whether or not they should consider supplier partnership:

1   Do bought-in products and services account, by value, for more than 50 per cent of your turnover?
2   Do you consider your suppliers as a source or potential source of competitive advantage?
3   Do you purchase or wish to purchase on the basis of total acquisition cost (rather than initial unit price)?
4   In three years' time, do you believe that your existing suppliers will fail to meet your needs and requirements in terms of:
    ● cost?
    ● quality?
    ● delivery?
    ● engineering and design expertise?
5   Would you like your suppliers to be more responsive to your needs?
6   Are you prepared to be more responsive to your suppliers' needs?
7   Are you prepared to treat your suppliers as partners in your business?
8   Do you wish to develop and maintain an open, frank and trusting relationship with your suppliers?

If you answered 'yes' to five or more of these questions then move on to Step 2. If your answer is 'no' to the majority of these questions, then the remainder of this chapter is probably not for you.

Step 2: Benefits and drawbacks

Establish a small subgroup of the senior management team to act as a supplier partnership assessment group. The remit of the group should be to carry out the tasks listed below, but the group should be free to draw information and assistance from appropriate sources as necessary. The investigation is basically for data gathering – to provide information for the senior management team to debate and discuss. It should be possible for the group to complete its remit speedily and with little need to call on additional resources.

The group's remit includes:

1   Examine the benefits and drawbacks which other companies have experienced with supplier partnership.
2   List five benefits of supplier partnership to your company.
3   List five drawbacks of supplier partnership to your company.
4   Ask the other members of the senior management team to state what they see as five main disadvantages or obstacles to supplier partnership.
5   Organize a half-day workshop for the senior management team to discuss, debate and evaluate the replies to the above questions. Then ask them to decide whether to proceed further with supplier partnership or abandon the concept.

Step 3: Developing an action plan

If the decision from Step 2 is to proceed, then it is necessary to establish a small, multidisciplinary project team to develop an action plan for the introduction of supplier partnership. There is no set formula for who should lead or be included in the project team. However, the presence of one or more senior managers signals support from, and provides a channel of communication to, the rest of the senior management team. Obviously, the purchasing function needs to be represented on the team, but so should other key functions and processes in the organization. Once the team has been established it should pursue the type of tasks which are outlined below. The list of tasks and issues is designed to stimulate ideas and debate amongst the project team. The project team should not treat the list as exhaustive or requiring 'set' answers. The intention is to allow it to explore in depth the practical mechanisms that must be put in place in order for the company to adopt the ideals of supplier partnership.

The tasks and issues:

1   Is the team looking at customer–supplier relations or should it be primarily concerned with the philosophy and operations of the entire company?

2   Does the project team feel that its remit is sufficiently wide and that it has the necessary authority to tackle the real issues involved? If the answer is 'no', the team must clarify and/or redefine its remit with senior management.
3   Who needs to be involved/consulted regarding the development and content of the action plan?
4   What should be the core values expressed in the company's supplier partnership philosophy?
5   Will this new approach to suppliers be consistent with the company's existing culture or should the company consider changing its culture?
6   How to evaluate suppliers and decide which to develop a long-term relationship with.
7   What resources does the company need to devote to supplier partnership?
8   Does supplier partnership require a multifunctional approach?
9   How to develop effective and consistent communications with suppliers.
10   How to build trust between the company and its suppliers.
11   What training courses can the company provide for its suppliers and vice versa?
12   Should the company establish an awards scheme to give recognition to its best suppliers?
13   How to consistently put into practice the company's supplier partnership philosophy.

The investigation of these issues should provide the information and ideas necessary to construct an action plan for introducing supplier partnership. The plan should be a written document which should be widely discussed and debated within the company and with key suppliers, before the senior management team decides whether to accept or amend its recommendations. Even at this stage, the senior management team should still be prepared to reject or delay the introduction of supplier partnership if the cost/risks appear to outweigh the benefits/potential and it is not right for the business at that time. The action plan format should include the following:

- a mission statement
- quantified objectives to be achieved after a significant period (such as five years) of supplier development with shorter-term (e.g. one year) milestones
- the resources necessary and the people responsible for implementing the steps towards supplier development
- the mechanisms for implementing the plan
- the future of the project team and who and what will succeed it
- recognition that there will be setbacks – a statement of commitment to resolving the obstacles and to keep the programme on course.

Step 4: Getting started

If the project team's report is accepted, with whatever amendments are deemed necessary, the organization should carry out the preparatory work for implementing the action plan as soon as possible. The first, and probably most important, step is to ensure that the company's own managers and employees understand the reasons for and become committed to the new approach to suppliers. Unless they are committed, it will prove almost impossible to win over suppliers.

Developing commitment

Most organizations will require a change of attitude and philosophy. There will be a need to convince people to accept the core concepts of supplier partnership, including:

- viewing suppliers as assets rather than liabilities or threats, and as partners not opponents
- recognizing that supplier partnership requires the establishment of long-term, frank and co-operative relationships
- moving away from purchasing solely on the basis of unit costs and instead adopting a total acquisition cost model which enables the company to identify the true cost of doing business with each of its suppliers.

moving away from unit costs to total cost of doing business with their suppliers.

Ivor Vaughan, the chairman of Rearsby Automotive, insists that everyone in the firm should use a simple guiding principle in their internal and external customer–supplier relationships: 'Don't treat anyone else in a way that you wouldn't want to be treated yourself'. He has found that changing the relationships between customer and supplier firms in the way indicated is a difficult and time-consuming exercise, not least because managers, who largely set the tone, are frequently moved into new positions. Nevertheless, winning the organization's commitment to change often involves one senior person 'making a stand', often with no immediate evidence that the new approach will actually work. Such a vision should be clearly stated, and continually backed up with action until the whole organization comes to believe it.

Nevertheless, Ivor Vaughan believes that:

Some companies are simply not ready for supplier development. If, within their organisation relationships are adversarial they *should not* start this process. Culturally and organisationally, they will be unable to benefit from efficiency gains in their supply base because they do not have the necessary long-term *commitment* to supplier development or to the *training and development* required at all levels to get employees to work differently. In short, you must 'clean up your act' first. Your motto should be: 'Behave within as you would like it to be outside the organisation.' The greatest obstacle remains the gap between good intentions and *action*. There are too many firms preaching the gospel of co-operative relationships who revert to traditional methods at the first setback.

Anticipating problems

Even when the ground has been well prepared, companies need to appreciate that moving to more co-operative relationships is, to borrow a phrase from the quality management literature, a journey not a destination. As with all journeys, some parts will go smoothly but at other points management may wonder why they ever set out on this venture in the first place. Some developments will be particularly controversial. For customers, one of these is usually single sourcing – some people feel it leaves them

It's a journey not a destination!

at the mercy of suppliers. For suppliers, on the other hand, one of the main concerns is open-book costing. Their fear is that customers might use this information to reduce margins or play one supplier off against another, or that the data might get into the hands of competitors. Unless such worries are anticipated, and strategies for dealing with them developed, they can severely damage the partnership initiative. In the case of single sourcing and open-book costing, the answer is to see them positively, not negatively. Single sourcing signals very clearly to suppliers that they are entering a new era – the customer is showing in a very tangible way that trust exists. Open-book costing sends this signal back to the customers. It says, we trust you enough to reveal sensitive information. Many companies now use these and other methods; very few appear to regret it. For example, the Rover Group has moved towards new ways of doing business across all of its activities, under the Rover Group RG 2000 programme. Over the last decade Rover has steadily reduced its supply base. Most of its outsourced components are now single-sourced, which means that the initial sourcing decision becomes very important. When technology changes, for example, and there is a danger that the supplier will be left behind, Rover and the supplier in question will jointly face up to the implications (see Chapter 3).

Suppliers have to operate an open-book relationship and cannot keep their costs secret. All elements of a supplier's business can benefit from the elimination of waste which reduces costs. Under partnership arrangements, the stress has shifted from annual price increases to the continuous effort to reduce costs in customers and suppliers and this necessarily means providing suppliers with incentives to support such a process.

Summary

Changing relationships between one part of an organization and another is never easy. Changing relationships between organizations is even more difficult. It is not something which should be embarked upon lightly nor abandoned easily. If a supplier partnership programme fails, suppliers are unlikely to give the organization another chance. Remember the following rules:

- *Don't* begin unless the senior management team understands what it is letting itself in for.
- *Don't* begin unless the senior management team fully and openly supports supplier development.
- *Don't* begin unless you can gain the commitment of the rest of the organization.
- *Do* match actions to words.
- *Do* ensure there is some early and well publicized success.
- *Do* anticipate problems but ...
- *Do* expect success.

Further reading

Burnes, B. and New, S. (1996), *Strategic Advantage and Supply Chain Collaboration: Determining the Way Forward for Your Organisation*, A.T. Kearney, London.
Partnership Sourcing Ltd (1991), *Partnership Sourcing*, London.

7 Developing the partnership concept for the future

Bernard Burnes and Steve New

The sheer scale of the potential for improvement through the partnership approach is both an opportunity and a threat. The opportunity is for organizations to work together to improve service, expand market share and increase profitability. The threat is that the diversity of opportunities can fragment effort, suck in resources and reduce effectiveness. Therefore, the benefits that appropriate, well-thought out and well-managed customer–supplier partnerships can bring are considerable. Unfortunately, much of what has been written and spoken about partnerships does not distinguish between those situations where partnerships are possible and beneficial and those where they are not. Just as organizations operated a great variety of practices with their customers and suppliers in the past (not all of which could be classed as antagonistic), partnership arrangements come in all shapes and sizes, and emerge for many reasons, even within the same companies. Companies need to look beyond simple and attractive definitions of partnership and determine what is best for them in a particular situation, given the needs and capabilities of their customers and their suppliers. However, this does not always happen.

Many companies have and are declaring that they want partnerships with their suppliers and customers. In some cases senior managers spend much time talking to each other and their opposite numbers in suppliers and customers. They develop elaborate strategies for working more closely with their suppliers and customers, yet, in many instances, there is no apparent change at the operational level. Their marketing and purchasing departments still, to all intents and purposes, operate in the same old adversarial, win–lose fashion. On the other hand, regardless of whether senior managers favour partnerships or not, there are also instances where, at an operational level, the logistics managers from customers and suppliers operate an unofficial partnership out of necessity.

Clearly both approaches are sub-optimal and arise from a failure to appreciate the benefits and difficulties entailed in establishing partnerships, especially the need for a consistent approach throughout the organization. What is required, if partnerships are to achieve their purpose, is a combination of strategic intent and operational necessity. However, not all customers want or can achieve a partnership with all their suppliers. Similarly, not all suppliers want or can achieve a partnership with their customers. Choice, for a variety of reasons, is constrained and not everyone has a free hand in choosing their customers or suppliers. In many instances the range of customers/suppliers is very narrow and in others customers/suppliers may be imposed on an organization by a third party. Most organizations face a choice between those with whom they want to do business and those with whom they need to do business. In both categories there will be those who want to establish partnerships and those who do not. Organizations are faced with developing approaches to their customer/supplier base which are appropriate, well-thought out and well-managed but which recognize that it is not possible to work in the same manner with all customers and suppliers. This attitude does not invalidate the partnership concept, but it recognizes that companies in effect operate multiple partnerships and not all such partnerships are the same. By conscious decision companies will treat some customers and suppliers differently from others. This chapter explores the type of issues which organizations need to consider in deciding their approach to partnership.

Identifying the basics

There are three basic questions which need to be addressed in order to identify the most suitable approach to partnership:

1 How can an organization determine its objectives for its customers/suppliers?
2 What forms of partnership exist to meet these objectives and what benefits do they produce?
3 How can the approach be operationalized and the benefits measured?

With regard to the first question, customer/supplier strategies must be consistent with and help to achieve an organization's strategic objectives, whilst at the same time meeting its operational needs. Given that every company has a different combination of strategic objectives and operational needs, it follows that companies cannot afford to adopt, unquestioningly, a standard approach to partnership. Rather the approach must be tailored to the particular needs of each organization.

It is clear, over the last decade or so, that most customers have moved their focus away from merely one aspect of the relationship with suppliers (i.e. price) and are concerned with the overall level of service that suppliers are or should be delivering. In turn this has not only laid great stress on companies rearranging (or re-engineering) their internal arrangements and processes to increase the level of service to customers, it has also focused attention on the type of relationship they want/need with their suppliers/customers. The move to service rather than just price is significant, but 'price' has not necessarily decreased in importance, rather other factors have been added to it (cost, delivery, quality, design, development potential, etc.) to achieve a view of the total cost of the relationship both in the short and medium term. The broadening out of the purchasing/selling criteria and the fact that the mix changes from organization to organization (and even within the supplier/customer base in the same organization), and over time, is one of the main reasons why there appears to be such a variety of partnerships emerging.

Three approaches to partnership

Three basic approaches to partnership have been identified:

- co-operation
- supplier development
- survival of the fittest.

Co-operation

Under the co-operation approach, supply chain improvement is achieved by firms working to remove the waste generated at the interface between customers and suppliers. It is the standard model of partnership sourcing and leads to the general con sion that more trust is needed to improve industrial per mance. The objective is for customers and suppliers to striv substitute co-operation for conflict and in so doing reduce cost of transacting business with each other.

This approach has given rise to a number of interesting de opments. The obvious one is the move to single sourcing, wl allows both customers and suppliers to focus on develor approaches to their joint business which bring mutual benefit, I in the long and short term. One other such development, wl holds out much promise for cost reduction and revenue gen tion, is vendor-managed inventory (VMI). Though isolated ex ples of this have been around for some time, it is now becon more prevalent. In the car industry a number of Nissan's UK pliers have been delivering to the track side for some years an the food industry Nestlés are now managing the inventory i number of their wholesale customers. There are consider advantages for both customers and suppliers to the appro However, the biggest barrier to an increase in the use of VMI similar approaches is the perception amongst customers and pliers that it is open to abuse, which is why the issue of tru important. Nevertheless, trust cannot exist in a vacuum and important that it is supported by systems which allow both tomers and suppliers to verify and feel safe with such arrangements. Somerfield Stores have developed their own variant of VMI which they call co-managed inventory (CMI). It recognizes the fact that customers still play an important role in inventory management. In piloting this approach, Somerfield have taken great pains to ensure that the necessary computer systems were developed which allowed them to monitor and, if necessary, intervene in the inventory management process (see Burnes and New, 1996).

Supplier development

The second approach has as its essence an active partner (the customer) who puts resources in to improving its suppliers. It is most prevalent in the motor industry and was introduced into the UK by Nissan in the late 1980s (see Lloyd et al., 1994). Nissan operates a supplier development team (SDT) whose remit is to work with suppliers to improve its business. Originally the SDT directed its activities at shopfloor improvement, but has now broadened its scope considerably and even offers a strategy development programme to suppliers. The supplier development approach goes much further than looking at joint activities to reduce boundary costs and attempts (in its more extensive forms) to assist suppliers in an wholesale assessment and rebuilding of their business.

As with the co-operation approach, trust is vital (especially by the supplier who is expected to open up all areas of its business to inspection). However, once again the approach must be buttressed by mechanisms that reduce the fear that the customer will in some way abuse its position – one such mechanism is single sourcing and/or long-term contracts. Such an approach requires a wide degree of expertise from the customer (who in effect is offering a consultancy service to their suppliers) and a large resource commitment. It is also important that the customer is seen to have adopted best practice before trying to tell suppliers how to run their business.

Survival of the fittest

For many companies this is the most attractive approach. The customer/supplier concentrates on becoming the 'best in class' and chooses to work only with other companies which are excellent. In such a situation there is no need to have joint activities between customers and suppliers for mutual improvement because each, by pursuing their own path to excellence, is assisting the other. It is very much a case of like attracting like. The partnership between IBM and Microsoft to develop the MS DOS operating system for personal computers is a good example of this (see Burnes and New, 1996).

Each of these three approaches has a particular set of tools, techniques and organizational arrangements associated with it. If companies determine that their strategic interests are best served by reducing transaction costs, they would be diluting their effort in this area by establishing supplier development initiatives. The same argument applies to those organizations which adopt the third approach, survival of the fittest. Likewise, if an organization is committed to approaches one or two but continues to 'shop around' for the best suppliers/customers, then this will be counterproductive to the activities it is undertaking with existing suppliers. Nevertheless, it is not sufficient just to choose the most appropriate approach. It is also necessary to monitor its effectiveness to ensure that the anticipated benefits are actually achieved. The attractions and drawbacks of these approaches are summarized in Figure 7.1.

The three approaches are not the only ones available, though it is argued that they do appear to cover most of the key variants. One of the main reasons for distinguishing between them is that it allows companies to make sense of

	Pros	Cons
Co-operation	Eliminates interface waste	Doesn't tackle basic competence
Supplier development	Improves supplier performance	Resource implications and improved suppliers for competitors
Survival of the fittest	Requires few resources and has immediate impact	Assumes 'perfect' suppliers exist

Figure 7.1   The three approaches to partnership – pros and cons

what they are doing and why in some cases the anticipated benefits are not being achieved. Organizations can fall into the trap of attempting to do everything because they fail to identify in sufficient detail the needs and abilities of their individual customers/suppliers. In other instances, because the concept of partnership is so fuzzy, it is assumed that any of these activities will/must contribute to developing partnerships and improving performance. The main likely cause of failure is that companies do not link their strategic objectives to their customer/supplier strategies and consider the operational consequences of this.

Selecting an approach and measuring the benefits

Organizations need to consciously select the approach to partnership which best suits their needs and pursue it in a constant and systematic manner. Consequently they have to understand the particular package of tools and techniques which best deliver the benefits they require. It also means that organizations should be able to measure the benefits of their approach to partnership.

There are four steps that organizations need to take to develop effective partnerships:

1 Identify their own strategic needs.
2 Embody these needs in a purchasing/marketing strategy which identifies the appropriate approach to their customers/suppliers.
3 Ensure that this approach is consistently applied and that the appropriate tools and techniques are utilized.
4 Measure the benefits.

Underpinning these four steps is the need to recognize that few organizations have a customer/supplier base which exhibits uniform needs and abilities. Therefore, whilst companies should avoid using more than one approach with each individual customer/supplier, many companies will need to utilize more than one approach across their customer/supplier base.

The supply chain improvement process

In the future an increased use of partnerships is highly likely, given their many benefits. However, organizations need to recognize that different situations require different approaches. Also, partnerships must be based on a clear set of measurable goals which are linked to the organization's strategic needs and which utilize the appropriate tools and techniques to achieve these needs. An organization's customer/supplier base may have to be segmented so that each segment is dealt with in the most appropriate way, whether through partnership-type approaches or more adversarial relationships.

To achieve this segmentation, organizations must have a clear view of the supply chain improvement process and be able to identify where they fit in and the approach or approaches best suited to them. One such approach can be based on the Deming cycle of plan, do, study, act:

- plan – determine the approach
- do   – put it into operation
- study – measure the benefits
- act   – feedback.

In conclusion, the main requirement is that organizations decide consciously on the most appropriate customer/supplier strategy for them, rather than fall into one by default, and that they monitor its effectiveness and continuing appropriateness. They must understand the process of supply chain improvement and be geared up to pursuing it consistently. Organizations must also recognize the need to manage multiple partnerships. The message for the future is that an organization's approach to its customers/suppliers must be appropriate, well-thought out and well managed. This can only be achieved if organizations understand the process of supply chain improvement. In particular they must ask themselves:

- What are the most productive methods for working with our customers and suppliers to increased competitiveness?

- Are the three approaches identified in this chapter suitable for us and what other approaches exist?
- What are the full range of tools and techniques which accompany each approach and how can they be put into practice?

Further reading

Burnes, B. and New, S. (1996), *Strategic Advantage and Supply Chain Collaboration: Determining the Way Forward for Your Organisation*, A.T. Kearney, London.

Lloyd, A., Dale, B.G. and Burnes, B. (1994), 'Supplier development: a study of Nissan Motor Manufacturing (UK) and their suppliers', Proceedings of the Institution of Mechanical Engineers, 208, (D1), 63–68.

8 Customer–supplier relations – tools, techniques and systems

Barrie Dale and Bernard Burnes

It is clear from the preceding chapters that whilst developing partnerships has much to do with adopting a new approach/philosophy to purchasing and supply, there are a number of tools, techniques and systems which organizations can deploy in initiating, promoting and developing partnerships. The tools and techniques outlined in this chapter have been mentioned by the contributors to the book. Though some have been specifically created to aid the development of closer relations between customers and suppliers, e.g. supplier rating systems, most have been adopted from elsewhere, particularly the quality management field (see Dale (1994)) and the organization development field (see French and Bell (1990)). These tools and techniques, though suitable to many situations, can be grouped under three headings:

- those which assist an organization in 'getting started' on the road to partnership
- those which contribute to 'developing the benefits' from partnerships by continuing to improve the performance of both customers and suppliers for mutual benefit
- those which assist with 'monitoring the relationship' to

measure its efficiency and effectiveness and identify areas for improvement.

Before these three areas are reviewed, one proviso is necessary: organizations should only enter into partnerships with suppliers/customers when they contribute to their overall present and future business aims. It is assumed that the companies have some method of establishing these aims, whether the result is called a vision, strategy, mission or values. Unless organizations have some such method for identifying present and future goals, committing themselves to establishing partnerships may prove difficult.

Getting started

As outlined in previous chapters, there are no easy options as far as partnerships are concerned, but perhaps the biggest step to be made by an organization is to take the decision to move down this path. In considering this option, an organization needs to review its long-term objectives and establish how improved co-operation with suppliers might help achieve these objectives. The three techniques and tools which are most useful in this respect are: benchmarking, brainstorming and quality costing.

Benchmarking is useful because it enables the organization to compare its overall performance, especially the efficiency of purchasing processes and arrangements, with competitors and similar companies in other markets. Brainstorming, and its various derivatives, is an approach which senior managers can utilize to assess in an open and free-thinking fashion the benefits, alternatives and practicalities of partnerships. Quality costing allows the organization to identify the cost of poor performance from suppliers and thus judge the benefits that can accrue from more constructive relationships.

The use of these techniques and tools allows organizations to begin planning and implementing partnership programmes.

Benchmarking

Benchmarking as it is known today originated in Rank Xerox. It is well documented (e.g. Camp (1989)) that when Rank Xerox started to evaluate its copying machines against the Japanese competition it was found that the Japanese companies were selling their machines for what it cost Rank Xerox to make them. It had been assumed that the Japanese produced machines were of poor quality – this proved not to be the case. This exposure of the corporation's vulnerability highlighted the need for change which was led by David Kearns, who had just been promoted to the position of chief executive officer.

Benchmarking is defined by Rank Xerox as 'the continuous process of measuring products, services and processes against the strongest competitors or those renowned as world leaders in their field'. It was adopted by them in 1981 as a company-wide effort. Put simply, benchmarking is an opportunity to learn from the experience of others. Benchmarking helps to develop an improvement mind-set amongst staff; it facilitates an understanding of best practices and processes; helps to understand processes; challenges existing practices within the business, and assists in setting goals. It is used whenever it is necessary to share an approach, to change or improve business processes.

Most organizations carry out informal benchmarking in two main forms:

- visits to other businesses to obtain ideas to facilitate improvements in one's own organization and
- the collection, in a variety of ways, of data about the competitors. This is often not done in any planned way, it is interesting but limited in value.

To make the most effective use of benchmarking and use it as a learning experience as part of a continual process rather than a one-shot exercise a more formal approach is required. However, before an organization embarks on formal benchmarking it must be prepared to spend time understanding how its own processes work. This will often be the main criterion of the benchmarking activity.

There are three main types of formal benchmarking:

1   Internal benchmarking – the easiest form to conduct and involves benchmarking between businesses within the same

group of companies. In this way best practice and initiatives are shared across businesses.

2 Competitive benchmarking – a comparison against the direct competition. It is often difficult, if not impossible in some industries, to obtain the data for this form of benchmarking.

3 Functional/generic benchmarking – a comparison of specific processes with 'best in class' in different industries. Functional relates to the functional similarities of organizations, whilst generic looks at the broader similarities of business. It is usually not difficult to obtain access to other organizations to perform this type of benchmarking. Organizations are often keen to exchange information in a network or partnership arrangement.

There are a number of steps in a formal benchmarking process which are now briefly described. More detail can be found in Anderson and Petterson (1996), Camp (1989, 1995), McNair and Leibfreid (1993) and Zairi and Leonard (1995).

• Identify what is to be benchmarked (e.g. the invoicing process) and reach agreement on the measures to be used (e.g. number of invoices per day, per person).
• Identify which companies will be benchmarked.
• Agree the most appropriate means of collecting the data, the type of data, who will be involved and a plan of action.
• Determine the reasons for the current gap (positive or negative) in performance between the company and the best amongst the other companies in the exercise.
• Estimate, over an agreed time frame, the change in performance of the company and the benchmark companies in order to assess if the gap is going to grow or decrease.
• Define and establish the goals to close or increase the gap in performance. This step requires effective communication of the findings from the exercise.
• Develop action plans to achieve the goals. The plans must be accepted by all employees likely to be affected by the changes.
• Implement the actions, plans and strategies. This involves effective project planning and management.

- Assess and report the results of the action plans.
- Reassessment or recalibration of the benchmark. This should be conducted on a regular and systematic basis and involves maintaining good links with the benchmark partners.

Benchmarking is not an end in itself, nor is it an exact science. Nevertheless it does allow companies to compare the performance of themselves and their suppliers with that of other organizations and to identify where 'gaps' exist. They can then investigate why this is so and what action they should take.

Brainstorming

Brainstorming is a method of free expression and is employed when the solutions to problems cannot be deduced logically and/or when creative new ideas are required. It is used with a wide variety of tools and techniques. Brainstorming works best in groups. It unlocks the creative power of the group through the synergistic effect, e.g. one person's ideas may trigger the thoughts of another member of the group, and thus stimulates the production of ideas. The aim is to generate the greatest number of ideas in a short space of time. It can be employed in a structured manner in which the group follows a set of rules, or in an unstructured format which allows anyone in the group to present ideas randomly as they occur.

Consider the following factors when organizing a brainstorming session:

- Prepare a clear and focused statement of the problem.
- Form a group and appoint a leader/facilitator. A team will always produce a greater number of ideas than the same number of individuals working in isolation.
- Elect someone to record the ideas as precisely and explicitly as possible, ideally on a flipchart to maintain a visible and permanent record or on a white board.
- Review the rules of brainstorming (i.e. code of conduct), for example:
  - each member in rotation is asked for ideas
  - a member can only offer one idea in turn

- the ideas are stated in as few words as possible
- where a member has no ideas he or she simply says 'pass'
- strive for an explosion of ideas and build on the ideas of other group members
- accept all ideas as given and record them – ask questions only to clarify issues
- no criticism, discussion, interruptions, comments or judgement are made during brainstorming
- ideas are not evaluated during the brainstorming session
- good-natured laughter and informality enhance the environment for innovation activity
- exaggeration adds humour and often provides a creative stimulus.

- Review the typical difficulties encountered in brainstorming, in order to prevent or minimize their occurrence.
- Determine the best ideas by consensus. This can be done in a number of ways – majority voting or polling, Pareto voting, paired comparisons, ranking on a scale (e.g. 1–10), or each team member ranks the items in order of priority with 5 points given to the first idea and 3 and 1 points given respectively to the second and third ideas, etc.
- Write down the ideas suggested so that they can be seen by all members of the group.
- Allow the ideas to incubate for a period of time before they are evaluated.

In an organization with entrenched and possibly antagonistic views of its suppliers/customers, brainstorming can prove an effective way of exposing and breaking out of this mind set.

Quality costing
Considerable investment is required to introduce and sustain a process of continuous improvement. The majority of managements are not used to committing expenditure as a blind act of faith and will wish to check that the investment is cost effective. Quality costing can be used to make this assessment.

Quality costing expresses an organization's quality performance in the language of senior management, shareholders and financial institutions – money. Senior management may often be unmoved by quality assurance data, but are spurred into action when the same data are expressed and presented in monetary terms, particularly when the cost of quality as a percentage of annual sales turnover is of the same order as profit. Operators and first-line management will also react positively to quality initiatives when non-conformance data are presented in these terms.

The benefits of quality costs are related to their uses which are both numerous and diverse. They include:

- promote quality as a business parameter
- help to keep quality aspects of the business under the spotlight
- enable business decisions about quality to be made in an objective manner
- help to identify and justify investment in prevention-based activities, equipment and tooling
- educate staff in the concept of continuous improvement and thereby gain their commitment and reduce scepticism
- facilitate performance measurement
- identify products, processes and departments for investigation
- focus attention on the problems for which compensation has already been built into the system
- assist in setting cost-reduction targets and measure progress towards them
- provide a base for budgeting and eventual cost control.

The main approaches to quality cost collection are described by Dale and Plunkett (1995) and include:

- The list of cost elements typically described in BS 6143: Part 2 *Guide to the Economics of Quality*, 'Prevention, appraisal and failure model' (1990) and Campanella (1990).
- A list of elements can be developed from company-specific experience and the literature.
- The use of semi-structured methods such as: the process cost model outlined in BS 6143: Part 1, *Guide to the Economics of Quality*, 'Process cost model' (1992).

The elements identified from any of these approaches can be based on people's activities and/or material waste.

Once the cost of non-compliance is established, it is possible to identify the causes. Mainly those are usually the customer, the company itself and/or its suppliers. Given that up to 70 to 80 per cent of materials and services are bought in, clearly working with suppliers is one of the main methods for reducing quality costs. Acknowledgement of the fact that companies purchase some of their quality problems led to the American Society for Quality Control (ASQC) (now the American Society for Quality) producing a 'Guide for Managing Supplier Quality Costs' (1987).

Developing the benefits

Even when partnerships are established, after the first rush of enthusiasm where some significant benefits can be achieved, there is a need to work in a methodical, determined and continuous fashion to reap the full benefits. By their very nature the benefits can only be achieved by collaborative activity. Sometimes this collaboration can be in the customer's own organization, often it is at the interface between the customer and supplier, but most frequently it involves the customer working with the supplier to improve the supplier's own processes. The following tools and techniques are useful in this respect.

Activity sampling

The general purpose of activity sampling is to determine within a specified degree of accuracy the amount of time/frequency that is spent on specific tasks. It is carried out by making a limited number of discrete observations, rather than by observing the activity on a continuous basis.

The basic steps for designing an activity sampling study are as follows:

- Decide on the activities to be studied.
- Carry out a pilot study to identify the elements of work.
- Plan the survey. Brief those carrying out the survey, the

observations to be taken, consult everyone concerned in the study, and ensure that the conditions are as normal as possible.
- Design an observation recording sheet and carry out a preliminary survey to estimate the proportion of time occupied by the activities being measured.
- Carry out the defined number of observations.
- Determine the percentage of time occupied by the activity.

Cause and effect diagram

The cause and effect diagram was developed by the late Kaoru Ishikawa (1976) to determine and break down the main causes of a given problem. Cause and effect diagrams are often called Ishikawa diagrams or 'fishbone' diagrams because of their skeletal appearance. (Figure 8.1 shows an example of a cause and effect diagram from Cerestar, Manchester, which deals with increasing the efficiency of dextrose production.) They are usually employed where there is only one problem and its possible causes are hierarchical in nature.

The effect (a specific problem or a quality characteristic/condition) is considered to be the head, and potential causes and sub-causes of the problem, or quality characteristic/condition to be the bone structure of the fish. Cause and effect diagrams illustrate in a clear manner the possible relationships between some identified effect and the influencing causes. They also assist in helping to uncover the root causes of a problem and in generating improvement ideas.

They are typically used by a quality control circle, quality improvement team, Kaizen team, problem-solving team, etc., as part of a brainstorming exercise to solicit ideas and opinions as to the possible main cause(s) of the problem, and subsequently to offer recommendations to resolve or counteract the problem. It is important to define clearly the problem or abnormality, giving as much detail as possible to enable the identification of potential causes. This can be quite a difficult task, and the team leader must assume responsibility for defining a manageable problem to ensure that the team's efforts and contributions are maximized in a constructive manner.

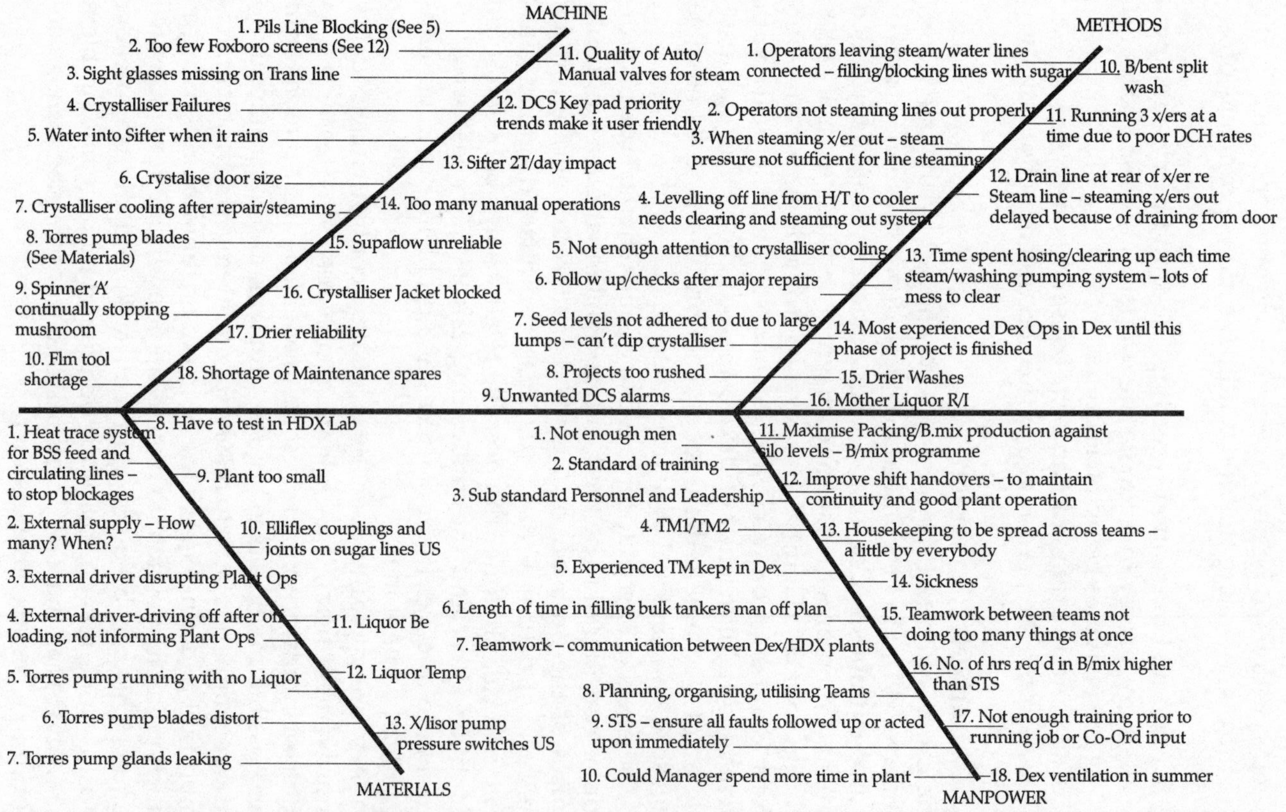

Figure 8.1 is a cause-and-effect (fishbone) diagram with four main branches: MACHINE, METHODS, MANPOWER, and MATERIALS.

MACHINE
1. Pils Line Blocking (See 5)
2. Too few Foxboro screens (See 12)
3. Sight glasses missing on Trans line
4. Crystalliser Failures
5. Water into Sifter when it rains
6. Crystalise door size
7. Crystalliser cooling after repair/steaming
8. Torres pump blades (See Materials)
9. Spinner 'A' continually stopping mushroom
10. Flm tool shortage
11. Quality of Auto/ Manual valves for steam connected – filling/blocking lines with sugar
12. DCS Key pad priority trends make it user friendly
13. Sifter 2T/day impact
14. Too many manual operations
15. Supaflow unreliable
16. Crystalliser Jacket blocked
17. Drier reliability
18. Shortage of Maintenance spares

METHODS
1. Operators leaving steam/water lines
2. Operators not steaming lines out properly
3. When steaming x/er out – steam pressure not sufficient for line steaming
4. Levelling off line from H/T to cooler needs clearing and steaming out system
5. Not enough attention to crystalliser cooling
6. Follow up/checks after major repairs
7. Seed levels not adhered to due to large lumps – can't dip crystalliser
8. Projects too rushed
9. Unwanted DCS alarms
10. B/bent split wash
11. Running 3 x/ers at a time due to poor DCH rates
12. Drain line at rear of x/er re Steam line – steaming x/ers out delayed because of draining from door
13. Time spent hosing/clearing up each time steam/washing pumping system – lots of mess to clear
14. Most experienced Dex Ops in Dex until this phase of project is finished
15. Drier Washes
16. Mother Liquor R/I

MANPOWER
1. Not enough men
2. Standard of training
3. Sub standard Personnel and Leadership
4. TM1/TM2
5. Experienced TM kept in Dex
6. Length of time in filling bulk tankers man off plan
7. Teamwork – communication between Dex/HDX plants
8. Planning, organising, utilising Teams
9. STS – ensure all faults followed up or acted upon immediately
10. Could Manager spend more time in plant
11. Maximise Packing/B.mix production against silo levels – B/mix programme
12. Improve shift handovers – to maintain continuity and good plant operation
13. Housekeeping to be spread across teams – a little by everybody
14. Sickness
15. Teamwork between teams not doing too many things at once
16. No. of hrs req'd in B/mix higher than STS
17. Not enough training prior to running job or Co-Ord input
18. Dex ventilation in summer

MATERIALS
1. Heat trace system for BSS feed and circulating lines – to stop blockages
2. External supply – How many? When?
3. External driver disrupting Plant Ops
4. External driver-driving off after of loading, not informing Plant Ops
5. Torres pump running with no Liquor
6. Torres pump blades distort
7. Torres pump glands leaking
8. Have to test in HDX Lab
9. Plant too small
10. Elliflex couplings and joints on sugar lines US
11. Liquor Be
12. Liquor Temp
13. X/lisor pump pressure switches US

Source: Cerestar, Manchester

Figure 8.1 Cause and effect diagram

120

There are three types of diagrams:

1   5M cause and effect diagram   The main 'bone' structure or branches typically comprise Machinery, Manpower, Method, Material and Maintenance. Often teams omit maintenance, and hence use a 4M diagram, whilst others may add a sixth M (Mother Nature) and so use a 6M diagram. The 4M, 5M or 6M diagram is useful for those with little experience of constructing cause and effect diagrams and is a good starting point in the event of any uncertainty. In non-manufacturing areas the 4Ps (Policies, Procedures, People and Plant) are sometimes found to be more appropriate.

   As with any type of cause and effect diagram, the exact format is not as important as the process of bringing about appropriate countermeasures for the main cause(s) of the problem, particularly where the problem cannot be isolated to a single section or department.

2   Process cause and effect diagram   The team members should be familiar with the process under consideration. They map it out using a flow chart and seek to identify potential causes for the problem at each stage of the process. If the process flow is so large as to be unmanageable, the sub-processes or process steps are separately identified. Each stage of the process is then brainstormed and ideas developed using, for example, a 4M/5M or 6M format. The key causes are identified for further analysis.

3   Dispersion analysis cause and effect diagram   This is generally used after a 4M/5M/6M diagram has been completed. The main causes identified by the group are then treated as separate branches and expanded upon by the team.

Cause and effect diagrams are usually produced via a team approach and involve the following basic steps:

● Ensure that every team member understands the problem, then develop a clear problem statement.
● Clarify and write in a box to the righthand side of the diagram the main symptom or effect of the problem and draw a horizontal line from the left of the box.

- Decide the main groupings or categories for the causes of the effect, which then form the main branches of the diagram.
- In a brainstorming session the group members speculate on causes of the effect, which are added to the branches or sub-branches of the diagram.
- In a following session the causes are discussed and analysed to determine those which are most likely to have caused the effect.
- The most likely or main causes of the problem are ranked, by the group, in order of importance. This can be done by Pareto voting; 80 per cent of the votes should be cast for 20 per cent of the causes. (If, for example, there are 35 causes, using the figure of 20 per cent this gives each member 7 votes to allocate to what they believe are the causes of the effect.)
- Additional data is sometimes gathered to confirm the key causes.

Departmental purpose analysis (DPA)

The main aims of DPA are to ensure that department objectives align with company objectives, to facilitate the internal customer–supplier relationship, to determine the effectiveness of departments in terms of purpose, roles, responsibilities and contribution and to extend the improvement initiatives to non-manufacturing areas.

The following are the key steps in undertaking a DPA:

- Define the purpose and aims of the department, and check that they are consistent with the company's mission and vision.
- Draw up a list of the main tasks carried out within the department. Prioritize the tasks and agree them with departmental staff and confirm with line management.
- List the main skills and activities for each of the key tasks; a flow chart is a useful tool to assist with this. For each of the tasks, identify and list the customers and the suppliers.
- For each supplier identify what input they provide and from whom this originates. For each customer determine what output they receive and who receives it.

- Discuss the inputs and outputs received from each supplier and customer respectively, identify any irregularities and abnormalities and agree specifications for needs.
- Identify any non-added-value, i.e. activities and time spent on tasks carried out which do not meet customer requirements first time and on tasks which are not required.
- Draw up an action plan to achieve agreed specifications and to reduce the non-added-value time.
- Review the skill requirements to identify any training needs.

Design of experiments

Design of experiments are a series of techniques which involve the identification and control of those parameters or variables (termed factors) which have a potential influence on the output of a process, with the objective of optimizing product design, process design and operation, and limiting the influence of noise factors. Two or more values (termed levels) of these variables are selected and the process is run at these levels. Each combination or experimental run is known as a trial. The basic idea is to conduct a small number of experiments with different parameter values and analyse their effect on a defined output such as plating thickness. There are a number of methods of experimentation – trial and error (the one-at-a-time method), full factorial and fractional factorial.

The trial and error (or classical) method changes one factor at a time keeping all the other factors constant. The experiments are run until some optimum level is found for the single factor. Keeping this factor at that level, changes are made to another factor to find its optimum with the other factors being kept constant and so on. Assumptions are then made about the preference for the lower or higher levels for each of the factors. This approach is quick, familiar and easy. However, it is widely criticized, not least for the fact that no information is provided about any interactions which may occur between the factors being tested leading to poor reproducibility and for being inefficient, resource intensive and costly. In addition, it is not easy to hold, from experiment to experiment, the factors constant and this in itself creates variation.

The full factorial approach considers, all combinations of the factors. In this way all possible interactions between the factors are investigated and the best combination identified. This may be feasible for a small number of factors but even with, say, 7 factors at two levels, the minimum number of trials would be 2^7, i.e. 128. Despite the fact that both the main effects and interactions can be measured in a thorough and purely scientific manner the time and costs associated with running such a large number of experiments are usually considered to be prohibitive and are simply unrealistic in industrial situations. This problem may be overcome by the use of fractional factorial designs.

Fractional factorial designs assume that higher order interactions are negligible and consequently the number of trials are a fraction of the full factorial (i.e. ½ or ¼). However, they still have the disadvantage of requiring a relatively large number of trials. Design of experiments dates back to the work in agricultural research of Fisher in the 1920s and historically required a great deal of statistical knowledge and understanding. In the late 1970s the work of Genichi Taguchi on experimental design made what is regarded by many as a major breakthrough in its application (see Taguchi (1986) for details of his method). Taguchi, along with others (e.g. Plackett and Burman (1946)), developed a series of orthogonal arrays to address the size of the experiment and thus aid the efficiency of conducting fractional factorial experiments. For example, the number of trials for 7 factors at two levels would be reduced from 128 to 8. An L8 orthogonal array from an experiment carried out on the corrugator at Rexam Corrugated South West Ltd is shown in Figure 8.2. However, whilst economics in the design of experiment are achieved, there is an inevitable loss of information, usually of some possible interactions between factors. Despite this drawback most practitioners appear to favour the Taguchi approach. Not only are his methods cost effective and time efficient, but they also work. Taguchi promotes three distinct stages of designing-in quality:

- System design – the basic configuration of the system is developed, involving the selection of parts and materials and the use of feasibility studies and prototyping.

	Gap	Straw Unwind	Gaylord Heater	Fluting Shower	Liner Wrap	Small P/heat	Roll Pressure	Strength	Variation
Set 1	6	Off	On	Off	Off	Off	40	58.73	6.93
Set 2	6	Off	On	On	On	On	60	76.27	7.18
Set 3	6	On	Off	Off	Off	On	60	63.26	6.29
Set 4	6	On	Off	On	On	Off	40	67.07	7.53
Set 5	9	Off	Off	Off	On	Off	60	61.65	4.51
Set 6	9	Off	Off	On	Off	On	40	61.19	4.90
Set 7	9	On	On	Off	On	On	40	65.56	4.57
Set 8	9	On	On	On	Off	Off	60	62.73	5.41

(Grade: 17FKB4, Speed 140 M/min)

Figure 8.2   Corrugator design of experiments and test results   Source: Rexam Corrugated South West Ltd

- Parameter design – the numerical values for the system variables (product and process parameters – factors) are chosen so that the system performs well, no matter what disturbances or noises (i.e. uncontrollable variables) are encountered by the system (i.e. robustness). The experimentation pinpoints this combination of product/process parameter levels. The emphasis in parameter design is on using low-cost materials and processes in the production of the system. Parameter design is the key stage of designing-in quality.

  The objective is to identify optimum levels for these control factors so that the product and/or process is least sensitive to changes in the noise factors.
- Tolerance design – if the system is not satisfactory, tolerance design is used to improve performance (i.e. reduce variation) by tightening the tolerances on those factors which have the largest impact on variation.

His 'off-line' approach to quality control is well accepted in the West, particularly, with the engineering fraternity, but inevitably there are many criticisms to some of his statistical methods and rather surprisingly to the advocated philosophy. What the critics seem to forget is that Taguchi's methods have proven successful both in Japan and the West, and those organizations who have adopted his methods have succeeded in making continuous improvement; it is this which is important and not the methods used. There is little doubt that his work has led to increased interest in a variety of approaches and methodologies relating to design of experiments.

Failure mode and effects analysis

The technique of failure mode and effects analysis (FMEA) was developed in the aerospace and defence industries. It is a systematic and analytical quality planning tool for identifying, at the product, service and process design stages, what potentially could go wrong either with a product during its manufacture or end-use by the customer or with the provision of a service. The use of FMEA is a powerful aid to undertaking advanced quality planning of new products and services, since it assists in the development of robust and reliable production and delivery methods. Its effective use should lead to improved customer satisfaction and confidence in products and services and a reduction in:

- defects during the production of initial samples and in volume production
- customer complaints
- failures in the field
- performance-related deficiencies
- warranty claims

There are two categories of FMEA: design and process. Design FMEA assesses what could, if not corrected, go wrong with the product in service and during manufacture as a consequence of a weakness in the design. When used in this way it assists in the identification or confirmation of critical characteristics. Process FMEA is mainly concerned with the reasons for potential failure during manufacture and in service as a result of non-compliance with the original design intent, or failure to achieve the design specification.

From the design FMEA, the potential causes of failure should be studied and actions taken before designs and drawings are finalized. Likewise, with the process FMEA, actions must be put into place before the process is set up. Used properly, FMEA prevents potential failures occurring in the manufacturing, producing and/or delivery processes or in the end-product during use, and will ensure that processes, products and services are more robust and reliable. There is little doubt that a number of the product recall campaigns, which are well publicized each year, could conceivably be avoided by the effective use of FMEA. However, it is important that FMEA is seen not just as a catalogue of potential failures, but as a technique for pursuing continuous improvement. It should also not be viewed as a paperwork exercise carried out to retain business, as this will limit its perceived usefulness.

Details of FMEA are provided in Dale (1994) and Ford Motor Company (1988). A skeleton design FMEA from RHP Bearings is shown in Figure 8.3.

Potential Failure Mode and Effects Analysis
System FMEA

Bearing type
Bearing number
Customer
Application
Position
T.O. number

Design responsibility
Site(s) involved
Suppliers involved
Engineering release date
FMEA prepared by
Given number

Original FMEA date
Current date 15-Sep-97
Number of sheets
Comments
Acceptance sig

Row no.	Part name, number & function	Potential failure mode	Potential effect(s) of failure	Severity	Potential cause(s) of failure	Occurrence	Design verification	Detection	RPN	Recommended actions	Responsibility and completion date	Actions taken	Severity	Occurrence	Detection	RPN
1	ENSURE SAFE RADIAL LOCATION UNDER ROTATION (Product Internal Function)	Premature bearing fatigue	Vibration, noise		Incorrect material selection		Data sheets / Test / service experience									
2			Vibration, noise		Incorrect / inadequate surface treatment		Test / service experience									
3			Vibration, noise		Incorrect internal design		Test / service experience / Calculation									
4			Vibration, noise		Contamination		Understand with customer									
5			Vibration, noise		Insufficient / inadequate lubrication		Discuss with customer / Test / service experience / Calculation									
6			Vibration, noise		Excessive loads		Discuss with customer / Test / service experience									
7		Corrosion	Vibration, noise, contamination		Incorrect material selection		Data sheets / specifications / Test / service experience									
8			Vibration, noise, contamination		Incorrect packing or handling		Data sheets / Test / service experience									
9			Vibration, noise, contamination		Incorrect / insufficient surface modification or treatment		Test / service experience									
10			Vibration, noise, contamination		Incorrect / insufficient enclosure		Data sheets / Test / service experience									
11		Seizure	Loss of rotation		Incorrect material selection		Data sheets / Test / service experience									
12			Loss of rotation		Insufficient / unsuitable lubrication		Discuss with customer / Test / service experience / Calculation									
13			Loss of rotation		Incorrect internal design		Discuss with customer / Test / service experience / Calculation									
14			Loss of rotation		Incorrect / inadequate surface treatment		Data sheets									

Figure 8.3 Failure mode and effects analysis

Source: RHP Bearings: Aerospace

128

The procedure in the development of FMEA is progressive iteration. In brief it involves the following steps:

- Form a team. ← *How do you est an effective team?*
- Flow chart the details of the relevant part, product, service process which is under study.
- Identify the function of the part, product, service and/or process and enter onto the FMEA form suitable details of the part, product, assembly, etc. which is under analysis.
- Identify potential failure modes in the part, product, service, etc. Each potential failure mode for the part and part function should be listed, data on previous parts is a useful starting point.
- Describe and assess the effects of each potential failure on the customer (internal and external).
- Examine the causes of potential failure, with each cause assigned to a failure mode.
- Estimate the occurrence that a specific cause will result in the failure mode.
- Review the current controls and assess the ability to detect a potential failure mode in relation to potential design, service or process weakness.
- Determine a risk priority number (RPN). This comprises an assessment of (i) occurrence, (ii) detection and (iii) severity of ranking and is the sum of the three rankings:
  (i) Occurrence is the likelihood of a specific cause which will result in the identified failure mode and is based on perceived or estimated probability ranked on a scale of 1–10.
  (ii) Detection criterion relates, in the case of a design FMEA, to the likelihood of the design verification programme pinpointing a potential failure mode before it reaches the customer (a ranking of 1–10 is used). In the process FMEA, this relates to the existing control plan.
  (iii) Severity of effect on a scale of 1–10 indicates the likelihood of the customer noticing any difference to the functionality of the product or service.

The resulting RPN should always be checked against past experience of similar products, services and situations. After it has been determined the potential failure modes in descending order of RPN should be the focus for improvement action to reduce/eliminate the risk of failure occurring.

Corrective action to help eliminate potential concerns is recommended. This, along with the counter-measures which have been put into place, are monitored.

The concept, procedures and logic involved with FMEA are not new. Every forward-thinking design, planning and production engineer and technical specialist carries out, in an informal manner, various aspects of FMEA. In fact, most people in their daily routines subconsciously use a simple informal FMEA. However, this mental analysis is rarely committed to paper in a format which can be evaluated by others and discussed as the basis for a corrective action plan. FMEA provides a planned, systematic method of capturing and documenting this knowledge. It also forces people to use a disciplined approach and is a vehicle for obtaining collective knowledge and experience through team activity.

Flow charts

Process mapping (sometimes called 'blue printing' or process modelling), in either a structured or unstructured format, is a prerequisite to obtaining an in-depth understanding of a process, before the application of quality management techniques such as FMEA, SPC and quality costing. A flow chart is employed to provide a diagrammatic picture, by means of a set of symbols, showing all the steps or stages in a process, project or sequence of events and is of considerable assistance in documenting and describing a process as an aid to its subsequent examination and improvement. A typical example of a flow chart from British Aerospace Defence Dynamics is shown in Figure 8.4.

A chart, when used in a manufacturing context, may show the complete process from goods-receiving through storage, manufacture, assembly to despatch of final product or simply some part of this process in detail. It is important that each 'activity' is included to focus attention on aspects of the process or subset of the process where problems have occurred or may occur so that some corrective action can be taken or countermeasure put into place.

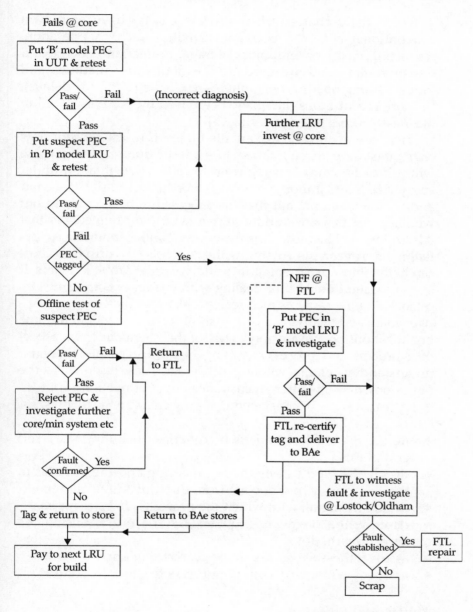

Source: British Aerospace Dynamics

Figure 8.4 Flow chart for Ferranti PECs – core failures

Traditionally charts (called process charts) have employed conventional symbols to define activities such as operation, inspection, delay or temporary storage, permanent storage and transportation, and are used by operations and methods and industrial engineering personnel (see Currie (1989) for details). In more recent times they have been used by those involved in business process re-engineering (BPR).

There are a number of variants of the classical process flow chart, including those tailored to an individual company's use with different symbols being used to reflect the situation under study. The most important point is not the format of the chart and/or flow diagram, but that the process has been mapped out with key inputs, value-adding steps and outputs defined and that it is understood by those directly involved and responsible for initiating improvements. Analysing the data collected on a flow chart can help to uncover irregularities and potential problem points. It is also a useful method of dealing with customer complaints, by establishing the cause of the break/problems in the customer/supplier chain and rectifying it by means of corrective action. In some organizations people are only aware of their own particular aspect of a process and process mapping helps to facilitate a greater understanding of the whole process. They are essential to the development of the internal customer–supplier relationship.

The main steps in constructing a flow chart are as follows:

- define the process and its boundaries, including start and end points
- decide the type and method of charting and the symbols to be used, and do not deviate from the convention chosen
- decide the detail with which the process is to be mapped
- describe the stages, in sequence, in the process using the agreed methodology
- assess if these stages are in the correct sequence
- ask people involved with the process to check its accuracy

Matrix diagram

A matrix diagram is used to clarify the relationship and main connecting points between results and causes or between objectives and methods and to indicate their relative importance. It is also used to draw conclusions between consequences and their causes and where there are two sets of factors and methods which may have no relationship with each other. The factors are arranged in rows and columns on a chart with the intersections showing the problem and its concentration, and identifying the base for future action and problem solving. Seeing, in graphical manner, the complete problem or picture with its essential characteristics and the impacting actions is of considerable help in developing a strategy for problem resolution. Symbols depict the presence and strength of a relationship between sets of data. There are a number of types of matrix diagrams (e.g. L-type, T-type, Y-type), each having a specific range of applications. Figure 8.5 shows the structure of an L-type matrix reflecting design and customer requirements, as part of a quality function deployment (QFD) analysis, from the Xerox (UK) entity-wide customer loyalty programme.

The steps in constructing a matrix diagram are as follows:

- Decide the format of the matrix – L-type, T-type, C-type, X-type etc., and the characteristics, tasks, problems, causes, methods, measures etc. to be compared, mapped and displayed.
- Decide how to arrange the problems and their causes. For example, in an L-shaped matrix for relating customer needs and design features the customer needs are listed in the rows and the design features relating to each need are listed in the columns.
- Define and specify the symbols which are to be used to summarize a relationship.
- Identify and discuss the relationships between, say, the needs and features or problems and causes etc. and use symbols to indicate the strength of the relationship where a column and row intersects.
- Review the completed diagram.

The main purpose of a matrix diagram is to identify problems and concerns and to enable corrective action to be implemented which

Quality Functional Deployment (QFD) – Project One Account Mgt
Goal: Deliver Co Wide Account Mgt to the Customer

HOUSE OF QUALITY:
Relationship
Needs vs Features
Strong +
Med ★
Weak ●

HOW

WHAT

Tasks (Design requirements)

HOW — design requirements (columns):
- Accountable lead for each account
- Enable bring in expertise/knowledge
- Align service and admin to account mgt
- Build account handover procedures
- Develop coverage plan acct by acct/territory
- Develop acct mgt/planning documents
- Develop longer-term planning cycle (3 yr)
- Build tenure mgt process by acct type
- Develop training in acct mgt co wide
- Territory/acct planning/sign off/review/coaching
- Align targets to acct/territory mgt strategy
- Develop appropriate set (broader) of territory goals
- Develop mgt system across functional boundaries

Target values/Operating system

WHAT — Tasks:
1. Provide account ownership
2. Provide single point of contact
3. Reduce fragmented dealings
4. Provide customer calling cycle
5. Address short-term planning
6. Improve continuity of contact
7. Employee capability to mgr C.C.C.

WHY:
- Weighting 1–5
- Customer experience
- Employee motivation
- Increased productivity
- Accountability
- Cost effective

WHY weightings (value 5):
- Customer experience: tasks 1 and 7
- Employee motivation: task 6
- Increased productivity: tasks 5 and 6
- Accountability: task 2
- Cost effective: task 3

Figure 8.5   L-type matrix diagram for customer loyalty programme   Source: Xerox (UK)

134

prevents them from arising again. Sometimes it is obvious where the fault lies but often, particularly where it may span the cus-tomer–supplier interface, it is difficult to identify cause and effect. In such cases, a matrix diagram approach can be highly beneficial.

Quality function deployment

The quality function deployment methodology was developed in Japan at Kobe Shipyard, Mitsubishi Heavy Industries. It arose out of a need to achieve simultaneously a competitive advantage in quality, cost and delivery (QCD). All the leading companies in Japan use QFD. It is based on the philosophy that the 'voice of the customer' drives all company operations. The technique seeks to identify those features of a product or service which sat-isfy the real needs and requirements of customers. This analysis also takes into account discussions with the people who use the product, to obtain data on the following issues:

- What do you feel about existing products?
- What bothers you?
- What features should new products have?
- What do you require to satisfy your needs, expectations, thinking and ideas?

It is usual to express the customer needs in their original words and then translate these needs into the technical language of the organization. Organizations use QFD to identify product and service features (including additional features) which customers will find attractive. In this way differentiating quality character-istics, features and/or technical advantages can be established between the organization and its competition. These features and specifications are then translated into design requirements and subsequently deployed through each phase in the 'manu-facturing' cycle to ensure that what is delivered to the customer truly reflects his/her wants or needs. It provides the mechanism to target selected areas where improvement would enhance competitive advantage.

QFD is a systematic procedure to help build in quality in the upstream processes and in the early stage of new product development. It helps to avoid problems in the downstream production and delivery processes and shortens the new product/service development time. It promotes pro-active rather than re-active development.

Some important issues have to be dealt with before QFD can be used:

- Decide which functions should be represented on the team and who is to be team leader, at the product planning stage.
- Overcome the usual comment of team members that they are too busy to attend team meetings, so that the team fails to meet on a regular basis. The need for good teamwork practices should also be recognized.
- Ensure that the supporting tools and techniques are in place.

QFD employs a step-by-step approach from customer needs and expectations through the four planning phases of:

- product planning
- product development
- process planning
- production planning through to manufactured products and delivered services.

In endeavouring to meet the objective of delighting the customer, conflicting issues often arise and some trade-offs are made in a logical manner.

In simple terms, QFD comprises four phases:

1   The project to be studied should be identified and defined by management. The scope of the project should be clearly outlined, including targets and operating constraints. From this a clearly defined mission statement should be produced.

2   Translate customer objectives and 'wants' (termed a what) into product or service design 'hows' (i.e. the product planning and design concept – phase 1). This 'voice of the customer' is the starting point for QFD and drives the process. Comparative analysis is performed between competitive

products and/or services, which helps to rate the importance of each customer want (the output from this rating process is termed 'whys'). There may be conflicts between customer 'wants' and design requirement 'hows'. The central relationship matrix of the chart represents the relationship strength of each customer need (whats) with each of the design requirements (hows). These conflicts are prioritized and a trade-off is made in terms of the addition and/or modification of product requirements. A 'how much' is established for every 'how' and target/specification values set. The design features' interactions are analysed in the roof of the house. Technical comparisons are made against the design requirements, both from the company's existing product and also from the viewpoint of competitive ones under investigation. This could involve some revision of the target value of the design feature.

3   Design requirements are then deployed to the next phase in the manufacturing cycle (i.e. product development and detail design – phase 2), again any conflicts are prioritized and trade-offs agreed and made.

4   The analysis is continued throughout the complete process of manufacture to delivery and even after-sales (i.e. process planning and production planning – phases 3 and 4). In this way technology restraints, and reliability and quality assurance control points are identified.

The analysis is progressive and can be stopped at any of the four phases. However, the experience from the Japanese companies is that the greatest benefit is derived when all phases are completed. A multidisciplinary team is used to prepare the QFD. The membership of the team is likely to change depending on the stage of QFD being addressed.

The use of QFD not only allows the supplier to meet (or even exceed) a customer's expectations but it can also force customers to define more clearly what it is they really want. Figure 8.6 shows an example from Allied Signal Turbochargers of the 'house of quality' derived from the product planning phase of QFD.

I. PRODUCT PLANNING

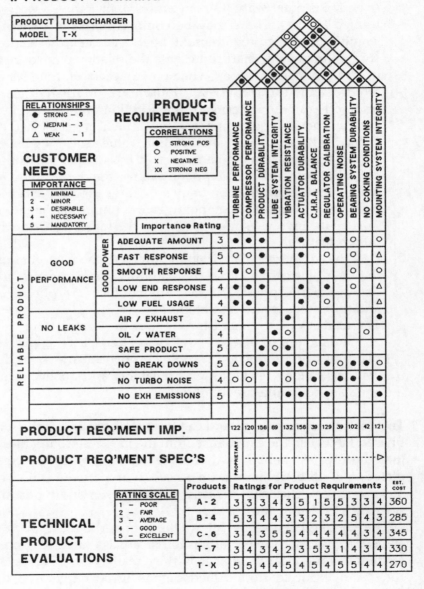

Source: Allied Signal Turbochargers

Figure 8.6   Quality function deployment analysis

Quality management system

The purpose of a quality system is to establish a framework of reference points to ensure that every time a process is performed the same information, methods, skills and controls are used and applied in a consistent manner. A quality system can contribute to both getting started on partnership and developing the benefits. Three levels of documentation, which is hierarchical in nature, are required as follows:

1   Company quality manual – the fundamental document which provides a concise summary of the quality policy and quality system along with the company objectives and its organization. ISO 10013 (1995) provides useful guidelines on the development and preparation of quality manuals.
2   Procedures manual – describes how the system functions and the structure and responsibilities in each department.
3   Work instructions, specifications, methods of performance and detailed methods for performing work activities.

In addition there should be a database (level 4) containing all other reference documents, e.g. forms, standards, drawings, reference information etc.

The quality system should define and cover all facets of an organization's operation from identifying and meeting the needs and requirements of customers, design, planning, purchasing, manufacturing, packaging, storage, delivery, installation and service, together with all relevant activities carried out within these functions. It deals with organization, responsibilities, procedures and processes.

A quality system, if it is to be comprehensive and effective and cover all these activities and facets, must be developed in relation to a reference base against which its adequacy can be judged and improvements made. This reference base is a 'quality system standard', of which the ISO 9000 series of standards is the most well known.

The objective of the ISO 9000 series is to give purchasers an assurance that the quality of the products and/or services provided by a supplier meets their requirements. The series of standards defines and sets out a definitive list of features and characteristics which it is considered should be present in an organization's management control system through documented policies, manuals and procedures, which help to ensure that quality is built into a process and it is achieved. The aim is systematic quality assurance and control. It is the broad principles of control, in general terms, which are defined in the standards, and not the specific methods by which control can be achieved. This allows the standard to be interpreted and applied in a wide range of situations and environments, and allows each organization to develop its own system and then test it out against the standard.

The ISO 9000 series consists of five individual standards, i.e. ISO 9000, ISO 9001, ISO 9002, ISO 9003 and ISO 9004, divided into four parts: guidelines; model for quality assurance in design, development, production, installation and servicing; model for quality assurance in production, installation and servicing; and model for quality assurance in final inspection and test.

The standards have two main functions. The first is an introduction to the series which identifies the aspects to be covered by an organization's quality system. The guidelines contained in ISO 9000 and ISO 9004 cover quality management and their application. The second function defines in detail the features and characteristics of a quality management system that are considered essential for the purpose of quality assurance in contractual situations, for three main different types of organization, depending upon the services they offer. Organizations usually register for one of the following categories:

- design, development, production, installation and servicing – ISO 9001
- production and installation, and servicing – ISO 9002
- final inspection and test – ISO 9003.

ISO 9000 'Guidelines for selection and use' and ISO 9004 'Guidelines for specific applications' (which are considered as one part of this series of standards) consist of a number of parts and are intended only as guidelines. They cannot be used as reference standards with which to assess the adequacy of a quality management system. These two parts are more reader-friendly than ISO 9001, ISO 9002 and ISO 9003. Organizations embarking on the development of a quality system to meet the requirements of ISO 9001, ISO 9002 or ISO 9003, should find ISO 9000, 1–4, and ISO 9004, 1–4, of considerable help in the initial stages where an overview is needed.

ISO 9000–1   is a guide to the use of other standards in the series, and a thorough understanding of its content is essential if the series of standards are to be interpreted and used correctly.

ISO 9000–2   is a guide for the application of ISO 9001, ISO 9002 and ISO 9003. It helps organizations to understand the requirements of these three standards. It is structured in line with ISO 9001 and needs to be read in conjunction with that part of the ISO 9000 series with which compliance is sought.

ISO 9000–3   sets out guidelines to facilitate the application of ISO 9001 to organizations which are developing, supplying and maintaining software.

ISO 9000–4   is a guide to dependability (i.e. reliability, maintainability and availability) programme management and covers the essential features of such a programme.

ISO 9004–1   is a guide to good quality management practice and provides more detail than ISO 9001, ISO 9002 and ISO 9003. It also refers to a number of quality aspects (e.g. quality risks, costs, product liability and marketing) which are not covered in the same level of detail in ISO 9001, ISO 9002 and ISO 9003. Considerable emphasis is placed throughout on the satisfaction of customer needs and requirements.

ISO 9004–2   gives guidance and a comprehensive overview for establishing and implementing a quality system specifically for services.

ISO 9004–3   provides guidance on quality system elements for processed materials.

ISO 9004–4   gives guidelines for quality improvement, covering concepts, principles, methodology, and tools and techniques.

Statistical process control

Statistical process control (SPC), generally accepted as management of the process through statistical methods, has four main uses:

- to achieve process stability
- to provide guidance on how the process may be improved by the reduction of variation
- to assess the performance of a process and identify changes
- to give information to help management decision making.

SPC is about control, capability and improvement, but only if used correctly and in an environment which is conducive to the pursuit of continuous improvement. However, on its own, SPC will not solve problems. A control chart only records the 'voice of the process' and SPC may, at a basic level, simply confirm the presence of a problem. There are many tools and techniques which should be used prior to and concurrently with SPC to facilitate analysis and improvement. It is basically a measurement technique and it is only when a mechanism is in place to remove and reduce 'special' and 'common' causes of variation that an organization will be using SPC to its fullest potential.

SPC is now widely used in the UK and many customers see it as a method of assuming their suppliers can achieve the required quality standards. An example of a control chart for small batch runs from RHP Bearings, Aerospace is given in Figure 8.7. Montgomery (1991), Oakland and Followell (1990), and Owen (1989) discuss SPC.

Monitoring the relationship

In order to ensure that the process of partnership is achieving its objectives and particularly to identify those suppliers who require the greatest encouragement to make improvements, cus-

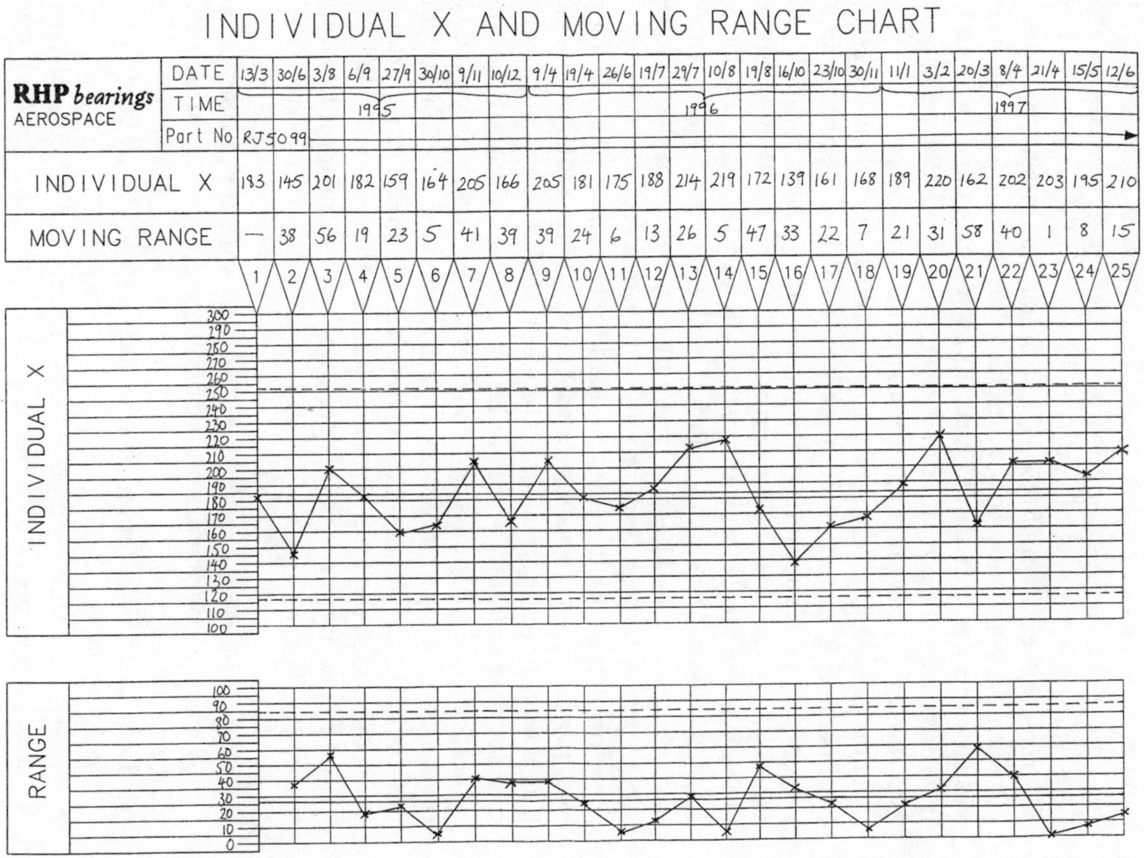

INDIVIDUAL X AND MOVING RANGE CHART

RHP *bearings* AEROSPACE — Port No RJ5099

	1	2	3	4	5	6	7	8	9	10	11	12	13	14	15	16	17	18	19	20	21	22	23	24	25
DATE	13/3	30/6	3/8	6/9	27/9	30/10	9/11	10/12	9/4	19/4	26/6	19/7	29/7	10/8	19/8	16/10	23/10	30/11	11/1	3/2	26/3	8/4	21/4	15/5	12/6
TIME	1995								1996										1997						
INDIVIDUAL X	193	145	201	182	159	164	205	166	205	181	175	188	214	219	172	139	161	168	189	220	162	202	203	195	210
MOVING RANGE	—	38	56	19	23	5	41	39	39	24	6	13	26	5	47	33	22	7	21	31	58	40	1	8	15

INDIVIDUAL X (scale): 300, 290, 280, 270, 260, 250, 240, 230, 220, 210, 200, 190, 180, 170, 160, 150, 140, 130, 120, 110, 100

RANGE (scale): 100, 90, 80, 70, 60, 50, 40, 30, 20, 10, 0

Figure 8.7 Statistical process control chart

Source: RHP Bearings: Aerospace

tomers must monitor the performance of their suppliers. Some of
the tools and techniques already mentioned are useful in this
respect, i.e. benchmarking and quality costing. However, one of
the most effective methods is a supplier rating system, which
allows a customer not only to monitor the performance of individual suppliers, but also to rank all its suppliers and thus identify those whose performance is up to and beyond expectations
and those who may be failing to come up to standard.

There are a wide range of rating systems; in the car industry,
for instance, every manufacturer has their own distinct system
which differs, sometimes considerably, from their competitors.
However, perhaps the most comprehensive and widely accepted
is the Nissan Motor Manufacturing UK Ltd (NMUK) QCDDM
system, which measures Quality, Costs, Delivery, Development
and Management. The first three of these are 'hard' measures
which relate to past and present performance. The last two –
Development, which relates to the supplier's ability to develop
new products and processes, and Management, which relates to
the ability, training and competence in depth of the supplier's
managerial personnel – are 'softer' measures but no less important. Most rating systems cover measurements relating to quality,
costs and delivery, but NMUK argues that a customer also needs
to look at future potential as well, especially given that partnerships are about the long term and not just the present.

The following three points are important in relation to rating
systems:

- They should be rigorous and provide sufficient information
  to measure performance and indicate present or future concerns.
- They must be accepted as fair and useful both by customers
  and suppliers.
- The information gained is fed back to and discussed with
  suppliers in order to achieve a common understanding and
  an agreement about future action and progress.

As well as providing feedback to individual suppliers, many
companies also publish an annual league table and offer awards

not only to those who outperform the rest but also to those who have made the most improvement over the past twelve months.

Conclusions

Building effective partnerships requires a change of attitude, philosophy and values by both customers and suppliers. It also requires an enormous amount of thought, analysis and hard work. This chapter has identified some of the most commonly used tools and techniques to assist with the process of partnership. The descriptions are not exhaustive and those readers interested in exploring tools and techniques in greater detail should consult texts such as Dale (1994) and Dale and McQuater (1997).

[handwritten: What is required]

It is important to remember that whilst customers and suppliers may be entering into unknown territory, others have been there before and have left a plethora of useful advice and information which, if utilised, can make the journey easier. Organizations should also be prepared to explore the literature outside of that of partnerships and purchasing in order to get a full understanding of tools and techniques.

Further reading

Akao, Y. (1991), *Quality Function Deployment: Integrating Customer Requirements in Product Design*, Productivity Press, Massachusetts.

Anderson, B. and Petterson, P.G. (1996), *The Benchmarking Handbook*, Chapman and Hall, London.

ASQC Quality Costs Committee (1987), 'Guide for Managing Supplier Quality Costs', American Society for Quality Control, Milwaukee.

Barker, T.B. (1990), *Engineering Quality by Design*, Marcel Dekker, New York.

Bendell, A.T., Disney J. and Pridmore, W.A. (1989), *Taguchi Methods: Application in World Industry*, IFS Ltd, Bedford.

BS 6143, *Guide to the Economics of Quality*, Part 1 (1992), 'Process cost model' and Part 2 (1990), 'Prevention, appraisal and failure model', British Standards Institution, London.

Camp, R.C. (1989), *Benchmarking: the Search for Industry Best Practice that Lead to Superior Performance*, ASQC Quality Press, Milwaukee.

Camp, R.C. (1995), *Business Process Benchmarking: Finding and Implementing the Best Practices*, ASQC Quality Press, Milwaukee.

Campanella, J. (ed.) (1990), *Principles of Quality Costs: Principle, Implementation and Use*, ASQC Quality Press, Milwaukee.

Currie, R.M. (1989), *Work Study*, Pitman, London.

Dale, B.G. (ed.) (1994), *Managing Quality* (second edition), Prentice Hall, Herts.

Dale, B.G. and McQuater, R.E. (1997), *Managing Business Improvement and Quality: Implementing Key Tools and Techniques*, Blackwell Publishers, Oxford.

Dale, B.G. and Plunkett, J.J. (1995), *Quality Costing* (second edition), Chapman and Hall, London.

Eureka, W.L. and Ryan, N.E. (1988), *The Customer Driven Company – Managerial Perspectives on Quality Function Deployment*, ASI Press, Michigan.

Ford Motor Company (1988), *Potential Failure Mode and Effects Analysis: An Instruction Manual*, Ford Motor Company, Brentwood.

French, W.L. and Bell, C.H. (1990), *Organization Development*, Prentice-Hall: Englewood Cliffs, New Jersey.

Ishikawa, K. (1976), *Guide to Quality Control*, Asian Productivity Organisation, Tokyo.

ISO 10013 (1995), *Guidelines for Developing Quality Manuals*, International Organisation for Standardisation, Geneva.

Lochnar, R.H. and Matar, J. E. (1990), *Designing for Quality*, Chapman and Hall, London.

McNair, C.J. and Leibfreid, K. (1993), *Benchmarking: a Tool for Continuous Improvement*, HarperCollins, London.

Montgomery, D.C. (1991), *Introduction to Statistical Quality Control* (second edition), John Wiley, New York.

Oakland, J.S. and Followell R.F. (1990), *Statistical Process Control: a Practical Guide* (second edition), Heinemann, London.

Owen, M. (1989), *SPC and Continuous Improvement*, IFS Ltd, Bedfordshire.

Plackett, R.L. and Burman J.P. (1946), 'The design of optimum multi-factorial experiments', *Bionsetrika*, 33 (3), 305–325.

Shingo, S. (1986), *Zero Quality Control: Source Inspection and the Poka-Yoke System*, Productivity Press, Massachusetts.

Taguchi, G. (1986), *Introduction to Quality Engineering*, Asian Productivity Organisation, Tokyo.

Zairi, M. and Leonard, P. (1995), *Practical Benchmarking: A Complete Guide*, Chapman and Hall, London.

9 Developing partnerships: epilogue

Bernard Burnes and Barrie Dale

One of the key points which stands out from the previous chapters is the wide diversity of partnership arrangements which have developed within the UK over the last decade. Though, as might be expected, there is a marked contrast between the public and private sectors, there is an equally marked contrast within the private sector, which is neither surprising nor any cause for alarm. The main driving force behind the move to customer–supplier partnerships has been the establishment of Japanese transplants in Europe, especially the UK. It has to be recognized, however, that the conditions under which European customers and suppliers operate are markedly different from those in Japan. In Japan many large organizations have dedicated suppliers – companies who only supply them. This has led to the phenomenon, in the motor industry for example, where it is not just Toyota vying with Nissan and Honda for supremacy, but the entire Toyota supply chain battling against the Nissan and Honda supply chains. These are clearly not the conditions which operate in the UK and the rest of Europe.

In the UK, dedicated suppliers are few and far between. The best and most competitive suppliers deal with most if not all the main companies in their industry. These suppliers work closely with a particular customer to develop a product, process or service. The way that this is done varies, but includes obtaining suppliers' input on product development and sharing product planning and development data with suppliers. However, the benefit to that customer is likely to be short lived because, in a commercial environment, the supplier has to offer this same type of research and development activity to its other customers in order to retain their business. On this theme of development and the concentration on core competencies by the major customers it is clear that many UK customers and suppliers now seem ready to abandon adversarial relationships in favour of more co-operative partnerships. They are attempting to fit these partnerships to their circumstances and needs, rather than merely copying what worked for Japanese companies in Japan; this is the right approach.

Customers and suppliers, in a relatively short space of time, are having to learn, adopt and adapt an approach to purchasing which has taken Japanese companies over forty years to develop. Quite rightly, different companies, industries and sectors are developing partnerships in their own way to meet their own needs and circumstances. No one enters into a partnership with their suppliers or customers out of any altruistic motive or wish to be 'nice' to them. Partnerships are driven by hard-headed business objectives, mainly the need to achieve/maintain competitiveness in an increasingly global and hostile business environment. For example, suppliers are being told that for an increasing amount of business they are expected to cut costs.

It must be recognized that customer–supplier partnerships are not an easy option or some sort of panacea, particularly when suppliers are expected to meet the global requirements of their biggest customers. Underlying the rhetoric of partnership are difficult choices, not only about whether to enter into partnerships and what type, but also, and perhaps more importantly, the internal upheavals involved.

This epilogue chapter brings together the key lessons from the previous chapters in order to assist organizations to establish successful partnerships. It covers starting and developing partnerships; it describes the partnership process, the difficulties that organizations encounter and concludes by offering a list of do's and don'ts for successful partnerships. Above all, though, it seeks to show how companies can adopt and adapt the partnership approach to their needs and priorities rather than offering a rigid model.

Putting your own house in order

Burnes and Whittle in Chapter 6 show the steps that organizations need to go through to decide whether to undertake a partnership initiative. Even when organizations have examined all the issues involved and decided that partnership purchasing is for them, they should not attempt to rush into building new external relationships and mechanisms until they are sure that the internal equivalents are appropriate and effective. In particular, senior management should:

- outline clear objectives for the partnership initiative and ensure that those involved understand them
- develop a strategy and plan to accomplish these objectives
- establish a procedure for deciding which suppliers to involve
- ensure that the philosophy of the organization is in tune with, or can be retuned to, the partnership approach to purchasing, especially the need for teamwork.

Though the above will not necessarily be achieved easily, in the first instance perhaps the most critical task for the company will be to refocus and restructure those aspects of its own operations which are crucial to effective supplier performance. In effect, the company must put its own house in order before it asks its suppliers to do the same.

The increasing complexity of the task of obtaining conforming supplies at the right time, at the right price and every time suggests that the conventional form and organization of the purchasing management function may no longer be adequate. Traditional staff structures based on tight functional groups have resulted in compartmentalized attitudes to suppliers which hinder supplier development. Companies will need to restructure their purchasing, quality and engineering departments to ensure that they have the right skills in dealing with suppliers, and that functional accountability and logistics are adequate for the task of supplier development. It is also important to establish a multifunctional teamwork approach to purchasing (see the Rover Group study in Chapter 3).

To be effective, partnership sourcing requires well trained personnel capable of helping suppliers achieve the objectives which have been agreed. Purchasing and other staff who, where necessary, liaise with suppliers will need to understand the capabilities of suppliers' processes and systems and have a good working knowledge of the philosophy, principles and techniques of improvement. It is also important that a customer's staff can speak the same language as their suppliers' counterparts, whether they be in production, quality, design, finance or sales activities. Embarking on an action plan for partnership with insufficient regard to the needs of the purchasing organization's skills is likely to result in frustration and possibly eventual failure of the initiative.

The most effective mechanism and linkages for communication and feedback need to be identified. Typically purchasing, quality, design, engineering/technical and production personnel all talk to suppliers, but with no single functional area accepting total responsibility for the quality, cost and delivery of the bought-out items. The need for clear accountability and co-ordination is an important factor in ensuring that channels of communication between customers and suppliers are effective. It must be clear who will be responsible for all negotiations and communications for current and future business with each supplier.

For a company with many suppliers and bought-out items it may take several years to introduce and develop an effective process of partnership. Not all suppliers will welcome or be capable of accepting a partnership approach. Some, for whatever reason, will prefer to maintain a more adversarial approach. Although in the longer term a process of supply base reduction will eliminate many, others may well remain. It will also be the case that whilst a few suppliers may be world class, the majority will need to improve if they are to meet the company's expectations. Therefore most companies will need to adopt different practices with different suppliers. In most cases a partnership approach based on a commitment to supplier improvement will be the order of the day. On the other hand, with those suppliers whose performance is already world class, it may be the customer who finds itself being improved. However, with some suppliers, relationships may remain antagonistic.

Therefore, before starting a process of partnership, a company will need to review its supplier base and identify those suppliers with whom it needs to work in the long term and the type of relationship it will be able to establish. As it will not be possible to launch a partnership approach with all its suppliers at the outset, the company will need to establish a mechanism for selecting the initial group of suppliers. One method is to concentrate on new products, product and process modifications and new vendors. Another approach involves the use of Pareto analysis to focus priorities by ranking bought-out components and materials according to some appropriate parameter, e.g. gross annual spend. The case study of Cosalt Holiday Homes in Chapter 5 summarizes how they have undertaken this task.

To assist their suppliers, some large organizations have documented the fundamental requirements for the control of quality and achievement of improvement. Some have even produced explanatory booklets. It is a condition of the purchase order agreement that suppliers must ensure that their product complies with these requirements.

Nevertheless, although assisting suppliers to improve is important, the delivery of non-conforming products from a supplier can often be attributed to an ambiguous purchasing specification and poorly detailed customer requirements. Purchasing specifications are working documents used by both customer and supplier and must be treated as such. The content of material and product specifications has become highly standardized, and usually includes such features as functional physical characteristics, dimensional details, reliability characteristics, methods of test and criteria for acceptance, conditions of manufacture, installation, storage and use, and so on. The purchasing department should review the accuracy and completeness of purchasing documents before they are released to suppliers. It is good practice to send these documents to the quality department for its comments prior to transmission to the supplier.

Just as suppliers can learn from customers, the reverse also applies. Suppliers are knowledgeable in their own field of operation and should be given every opportunity to provide a design input to the preparation of the specification. With the reduction in specialist technical staff in customer organizations, this is now a common occurrence. Suppliers will be more likely to accept responsibility for defects and their associated costs if they are involved in the design of the product or formally agree with the customer the specification and drawing for the part to be produced. This supplier input to the design process is a key factor in cost avoidance and reduction and helps to reduce the product development lead time (see Chapter 4, for example).

One outcome of partnerships is that an increasing number of large purchasing organizations are awarding more long-term contracts and contracts for the life of a part. Strategic sourcing, i.e. single or dual sourcing, is considered by many writers and practitioners to be a complementary policy which will inevitably contribute to a reduction in the size of organizations' supplier bases. The reduction in the supplier base results in benefits such as:

- less variation in the characteristics of the supplied product
- supplier quality assurance and purchasing personnel can devote more time to vendors
- improved and simplified communications with vendors
- less paperwork
- less transportation
- less handling and inspection activity
- less accounts to be maintained and reduced costs for both parties.

It is easier to develop a partnership relationship if the suppliers are in close proximity to the customer. Consequently, a number of customers are now reversing their international sourcing strategies to develop shorter supply lines and are recommending that suppliers set up operations close to their main manufacturing facilities. Closeness is also a vital element in the use of a JIT purchasing strategy.

The process of partnership

Having put its own house in order and selected suitable suppliers for inclusion in its partnership programme, the next step for the purchasing organization is to involve the suppliers and obtain their commitment. They must communicate to suppliers what is required and reach an understanding with them on a set of common objectives. The issues outlined by Burnes and Whittle in steps 3 and 4, Chapter 6, are useful checkpoints in this task.

The most practical way of setting about this task is to hold presentations to outline the following issues to suppliers:

- the approach to partnership
- the quality system standard to be used
- the assessment of suppliers' performance, how it will be communicated, what assistance will be provided etc.

Presentations to suppliers can be held either on the customer's premises or at individual supplier's sites. A supplier conference and/or presentation must give those involved an opportunity to air grievances and discuss problems in an open and honest manner and must be aimed at establishing a climate of co-operation and commitment.

Once a supplier's senior management team has agreed to participate in the partnership process, it is usual for the purchasing organization to visit the supplier's factory and carry out a formal vendor approval survey in order to assess the supplier's suitability as a business partner. The survey is a multidisciplinary task which may involve the customer's purchasing, quality, engineering and technical personnel. It should cover areas such as controls, workshop environment, plant, technology, research and development, quality systems, attitudes, responses, tooling, planning and administrative systems etc.

As part of its audit, a customer must assess the supplier's commitment to advanced quality planning. Advanced quality planning commences with a joint review of the specification and classification of product characteristics and the production of an FMEA. The supplier should prepare a control plan to summarize the quality planning for significant product characteristics. This would typically include a description of the manufacturing operation and process flows, equipment used, control characteristics, control plans, specification limits, the use of SPC and mistake proofing, inspection details, and corrective and preventive action methods. The supplier would then provide initial samples for evaluation, which would be supported by data on process capability on the main characteristics identified by both parties, plus test results. Following successful evaluation of initial samples, the supplier is now in a position to start a trial production run followed by routine volume production.

Once the customer has assessed the adequacy of the supplier's policies, systems, procedures and manufacturing methods, and the supplier has demonstrated the quality of his shipped product during some form of trial, the goods inward inspection of suppliers can be reduced considerably; in some cases down to the ideal situation of direct line supply. At this point 'preferred' or 'certified supplier' status can be conferred on the supplier. Many companies now operate a supplier award scheme to recognize excellent supplier performance.

This assessment should not be a one-off exercise. An increasing number of leading purchasing organizations will audit all their suppliers at regular intervals, thus ensuring that their systems, processes and procedures are being maintained and improved. The frequency at which each supplier is reassessed is dependent on such factors as:

- the supplier's performance
- the status awarded to the supplier
- the type of item being supplied
- the volume of parts being supplied

- the occurrence of a major change at the supplier (e.g. change of management, change of facilities and process change)
- the supplier's request for assistance.

The partnership process is ongoing, aimed at building up an effective business relationship based on openness – a relationship which demands a greater and quicker exchange of information between both parties. During the early days the parameters of the relationship are never completely clear to both parties and it takes time to work out ground rules which are suitable for the parties. Large purchasing organizations are encouraging electronic ordering and purchasing with their main vendors along with the electronic sharing of product data. This linking of information systems and processes can often test the strength of the relationship. The electronic data exchange relates to quality, technical requirements and specifications, schedules, manufacturing programmes, lead times, inventory management, and invoicing. Suppliers are obliged to communicate any changes to materials, processes or methods that may affect the dimensional, functional, compositional or appearance characteristics of the product. Customers are obliged to provide sufficient information and assistance to aid development of their suppliers' approach to continuous improvement. In some cases this extends to joint problem-solving and cost reduction activities. When the relationship has developed from problem solving to problem avoidance it indicates that a major hurdle has been passed.

It is argued by writers such as Fruin (1992) and Morris and Imrie (1992) that the benefits of partnership are best achieved by spreading the concept to all members of the value-added chain from raw material to end product. This is perhaps best handled by a supplier association, which is usually taken to be a group of first-level suppliers and a particular customer. This is a loose grouping who share knowledge and experience for the purpose of continuous improvement down the supply chain. It is characteristic of the Japanese supply chain where it is also usual for first-tier suppliers to develop their own supplier associations. Fruin (1992) points out that 'the Toyota Motor Corporation has three regional supplier associations and Nissan Motor has two'. These forms of co-operative supplier networks are now starting to develop in Europe. For example, Morris and Imrie (1992) describe a network in place at Lucas Girling, and Hines (1992) describes how the Welsh Development Agency through their 'Source Wales' initiative has assisted Llanelli Radiators to form a supplier association.

Potential difficulties of partnerships

In a partnership which is regarded as a success by both parties, everyone wins. If only one party is considered the winner, as is the case with typical adversarial purchasing arrangements, there can be no basis for a partnership. A partnership is about a long-term relationship between a customer and a set of suppliers in order to reduce total costs all round, develop and maintain a competitive position and satisfy the end customer. It is important that the partnership is lived in the way it is articulated and talked about. This is far from easy and there are many potential obstacles.

The following, based on our practical and research work, are the main difficulties usually experienced in developing a partnership approach:

- an over-emphasis on cost reduction and piece price down, rather than the total cost of acquisition
- variations in the approaches of individuals and a general lack of cohesion
- a perceived lack of understanding by the customer of the business implications of its actions, e.g. sudden and large-scale changes in production level and work mix, changes in priorities, and a failure to stick with delivery schedules
- poor and inconsistent communication
- unwillingness of the larger partner to reciprocate openness with the suppliers
- poor reliability of information and systems
- inadequate project management

- a tendency for the customer to blame all the problems on the supplier
- inability to respond to things which have gone wrong and to resolve the problem
- failure to respond to suggestions and ideas for improvement
- a lack of understanding from the customer of a supplier's constraints and problems
- a customer asking the supplier to do something which they themselves have not achieved
- a lack of understanding of the minor problems which undermine the creditability of the customer
- a mismatch between what is requested and the existing infrastructure.

Conclusions

Suppliers are now recognized as an essential part of any organization's competitiveness. There are two main reasons for this – greater global specialization and changes in the nature of competition. Effective partnership requires purchasing organizations to treat suppliers as long-term business partners and this necessitates a fundamental shift from the traditional adversarial buyer–supplier relationship. Properly implemented partnership will help to reduce costs and increase market share to the benefit of both parties, together with technology transfer issues surrounding product, process, practices, systems. However, the nature and mechanisms of partnership must be related to the particular circumstances and needs of those involved. In conclusion, the following do's and don'ts developed from the work of Galt and Dale (1990) will help both customers and suppliers to establish the type of partnership that is most appropriate for them:

DO

look at ways of reducing the size of the supplier base. By reducing incoming material, component and sub-assembly variability, outgoing product and service quality will improve.

ensure that, in support of the supplier development process and its various stages, your staff and those in the customer organization use the appropriate engineering quality tools. These tools include statistical process control, the seven quality control tools, the seven management tools, failure mode and effects analysis, fault tree analysis, quality function deployment, design of experiments; the tools also facilitate design for manufacturability and cost avoidance.

involve suppliers in new product development and investigate the full range of ways of achieving this.

encourage suppliers to despatch only conforming products, thereby eliminating the need to carry out duplicate testing and inspection on incoming goods.

award long-term contracts to suppliers who have demonstrated commitment and improvements in order to show tangible evidence of a long-term relationship.

consider implementing an assessment and rating scheme to select and measure the performance of suppliers. Poor selection will lead to increased costs as other suppliers are sought to compensate for the deficiencies of the one chosen without due care.

develop procedures, objectives and strategies for communicating with the supply base.

treat suppliers as partners, thereby establishing trust, co-operation and dependence.

ensure that the staff dealing with suppliers act in a consistent and courteous manner and match actions to words.

respond positively to suppliers' requests for information.

develop and decide upon mutually agreed purposes and values that define the relationship and measure its success. The approach by the customer must be seen by the supplier as helpful, constructive and of mutual benefit.

decide and agree on the best means of communication and the provision of reliable information and monitoring a constructive dialogue. Defined points of communication are recommended.

listen and be receptive to feedback and be willing to share information and ideas and discuss problems. Discover and respond to functional perceptions, in both customer and supplier, of the state of the partnership.

provide education to raise awareness of the partnership approach and specific training for the new skills required.

be honest on the state of the partnership and avoid complacency.

ensure that customer and supplier organizations are sufficiently knowledgeable about each other's business, products, procedures, systems and how the respective organization's work.

remember a flexible and open approach is crucial, with the encouragement of positive constructive criticism.

DON'T

begin partnership unless senior management understands what is involved and supports the concept.

overlook the fact that senior management commitment of both parties to the ideals of partnership is necessary along with its active participation in the process, including understanding its importance. Management must recognize that it is not a 'quick fix' solution to cost reduction.

treat suppliers as adversaries.

keep suppliers short of information.

buy goods on price alone. Criteria such as quality and delivery performance, R and D potential, competitive manufacturing and engineering excellence must also be taken into account.

constantly switch suppliers.

accept non-conforming goods.

talk quality but act production schedule and price per piece.

forget that the initial samples procedures is an important factor in receiving conforming supplies.

forget that the customer and supplier must be prepared to add value to each other's operations, through reducing costs, identifying opportunities for improvement.

forget that the change to partnering will take longer than expected.

overlook the fact that the principles and values of partnership must be cascaded to all relevant levels in customer and supplier and be fully accepted, in particular by those staff at the day-to-day contact point.

forget that the effectiveness of the partnership must be measured and monitored.

forget that developments affecting both parties should be carried out with mutual consultation.

assume that there will be no problems – suitable countermeasures must be ready to address the obstacles encountered.

Further reading

Dale, B.G. and Galt, J. (1990), 'Customer supplier relationships in the motor industry: a vehicle manufacturer's perspective', proceedings of the Institution of Mechanical Engineers, 204 (D4), 179–186.

Fruin, W.M. (1992), *The Japanese Enterprise System, Competitive Strategies and Co-operative Structures*, Oxford University Press, New York.

Hines, P. (1992), 'Materials management for the 21st century: Llanelli Radiators Supplier Association', *Logistics Today*, March–April, 19–21.

Morris, J. and Imrie, R. (1992), *Transforming Buyer–Supplier Relationships*, Macmillan Press, London.

Index

5M cause and effect diagrams 121

accountability 21, 23, 24, 34, 36, 68, 152
  financial 25–7, 34–5
activity sampling 118–9
added value 68
advanced quality planning 41
adversarial relations 22, 54, 73, 102, 152, 158
advice 6
alliances *see* partnerships
AQP *see* advanced quality planning
assessment of suppliers 41, 49, 53, 80–81, 96, 99, 155–8, 160
attitudes 2, 5, 67–9, 78, 80, 87, 97, 145
awards schemes 42, 64, 96, 144–5

bargaining 2, 6, 18
  see also negotiations
behaviour 2, 5, 14
benchmarking 5, 42, 45, 48, 49, 52, 57, 63, 112–5
  internal 113–4
benefits of partnerships 91–100, 101, 102, 107, 118–42
best practice (philosophy) 2, 45, 46–7, 49, 64, 66, 67, 105, 113, 114
bidding *see* tendering
blame free environments 88
bought-in components/services 1, 49–73, 76–7, 82, 85, 87, 94, 118
  see also suppliers
brainstorming 112, 115–6, 121, 122
BS 5750 standards 76–7
business effectiveness measures 47–8, 50, 53, 56–7
business practice integration 3, 4
business process re-engineering 132

cause and effect diagrams 119–22
CCT *see* compulsory competitive tendering

Central Unit on Procurement 23, 24
change 56, 60, 71, 77–8, 98, 113, 157
co-makership *see* partnership
co-managed inventory (technique) 104–5
co-operation 2, 9, 11, 14, 15, 16, 18, 19, 60–62, 92, 98, 104–5, 106, 112, 160
collaboration *see* partnerships
collaborative research 2
commitment 2, 7, 18, 51, 53, 78, 92, 97–8, 117, 160, 161
communication 3, 4, 24, 36, 76, 78, 80, 81, 83, 85, 87, 88, 95, 96, 114, 152, 154, 155, 158, 160
comparative analysis 52
competences 106, 150
competition/competitors 11, 17, 23, 40, 49–50, 52, 53, 60, 73, 85, 91, 93, 94, 108, 135, 136–7, 150, 159
  in the public sector 21–36, 47
competitive advantage 63, 77, 88, 135
competitive benchmarking 114
competitive tendering 7, 21–36
  for services 27–30
competitor products (evaluation of) 5
complacency 4–5, 52, 85
components 1, 59–74
Comptroller and Auditor General 25
compulsory competitive tendering 28, 29
conflicts 104
  in requirements 137
consensus decision making 81
continuous improvement 1, 2, 5, 7, 30, 36, 41, 46, 52, 53, 55, 64, 66, 69, 70, 76, 85, 93, 116, 117, 119, 126, 127, 157
contracting out of services 28–9
contracts 5, 21–2, 24, 26, 27, 31, 33, 34, 36, 105, 154, 160
  for local government services 28, 30
  in-house bids 27, 28, 34
Cosalt Holiday Homes 75–88
cost management 1, 3, 16, 22, 24, 29, 30,

31, 44–6, 47, 48, 50, 51, 52, 54, 57, 60, 64, 66, 68, 70, 71, 73, 76, 77, 86, 88, 93, 94, 97, 103, 104, 117–8, 135, 158, 162
sharing of cost data 15, 87, 99
targets 45
undercutting 2
see also value for money
credibility 3, 4, 5, 85
critical success factors 42
customer relationships 14
customer satisfaction 11, 50, 86
measurement 4–5
customer workshops 5
customer–supplier alliances *see* partnerships

data sharing 2
decision making 5–6, 81, 117
delegation 23, 67
delivery of supplies/products 3, 4, 30, 65, 67–8, 71, 73, 80, 93, 94, 127, 135, 136, 161
at Rover Group 39, 47, 50
at Nissan 64
Deming cycle (of planning) 108
Department of Trade and Industry 23
departmental purpose analysis 122
design of experiments (technique) 123, 160
design of products 3, 4, 5, 54, 57, 60, 66, 67, 73, 77, 88, 94, 137
at Rover Group 40–41, 47
cost factors 45
role of suppliers 3, 47, 60, 154
see also new product introduction process; research and development
dispersion analysis cause and effect diagrams 121
documentation for quality management systems 139
DPA *see* departmental purpose analysis
Drive for leadership (Ford programme) 64

EC public procurement directives 25, 35
EC Services Directive (1993) 27–8
EDI *see* electronic data interchange
effective cost management (technique) 44–5

effectiveness 101, 112, 122, 162
of equipment 49
efficiency 26, 30, 42, 54, 55, 87, 112
electronic data interchange 65, 67
employee involvement 42
empowerment 81, 85, 88
expectations of customers 42, 137

failure mode and effects analysis 126–30, 156, 160
failure of processes 126–30
fault tree analysis 160
feedback 4, 5, 87, 108, 144, 152, 161
see also communications
financial accountability 25–7
financial management *see* cost management
fishbone diagrams *see* cause and effect diagrams
flow charts 130–32
FMEA *see* failure mode and effects analysis
follow sourcing (Ford programme) 72
Ford Motor Company 60, 64
forecasting 24
fractional factorial designs method in design of experiments (technique) 124
fraud 26, 34, 36
full factorial method in design of experiments (technique) 124
functional/generic benchmarking 114

globalization 60, 64, 68, 71, 159
goals *see* objectives (of companies)
government departments (procurement in) 24

healthcare procurement 30–32
Honda (company) 73
honesty 2, 157

ideas 2, 68, 87, 96, 115–6, 119, 121, 159, 161
transfer of 3
in-house bids for contracts 27, 28, 34
information 6, 23, 27, 54, 70, 78, 94, 96, 99, 114, 123, 139, 144, 157, 158, 160, 161

innovation 4, 32, 47, 116
inspection of supplies 3
integrity 2, 52, 157
internal benchmarking 113–4
inventory control 3, 11, 16, 46, 49, 50, 71, 105
investment 3, 34, 50, 70, 117
Ishikawa, Kaoru 119
ISO 9000 (standards series) 8, 41, 76, 139–42

just-in-time distribution 55, 59, 86, 155

Kaizen *see* continuous improvement
knowledge 47, 54, 130, 157

L-type matrix diagrams 133
Latham review (1994) 22
lead times 11, 71, 73, 80, 87
leadership 44
lean manufacture and display (concept) 47, 49
learning 55–6, 113
legislation on public procurement 24–5, 27–8, 35
liability of products 67
Local Government Acts (1980, 1988 and 1992) 28
long-term partnerships 2–4

management 9, 10–11, 32, 42, 54, 62, 64, 68, 75–6, 80, 85, 86, 92–100, 102, 116–7, 144, 151, 155, 160–1
market research 5, 45
materials specification 24
matrix diagrams 132–5
matrix responsibility 68
measurement of performance 56, 64–7, 70, 108, 117, 142, 144
misconceptions 4, 6–7
mission statements 80, 97, 136
mistrust 67
misunderstanding 158
motivation 7, 86
mutual benefit 18

negotiations 2, 24, 25, 26, 29
Nestlé (company) 104
new processes *see* innovation

new product introduction process 45, 68, 69, 71, 93, 136, 160
see also design of products; research and development
NEXT 21 (Nissan excellence target) 72–3
Nissan Motor Manufacturing (UK) 62, 64, 91, 104, 144
non-conforming supplies 6, 154, 161
NX96 (Nissan excellence target) 66, 72–3

objectives (of companies) 41, 51, 55, 57, 66, 103, 108, 112, 113, 114, 122–3, 151, 155, 160
misguided 4, 5
open book costing 47, 52, 99
openness in relationships 94, 157, 158, 161
see also honesty
operational needs 103
organizational cultures 52, 57, 68, 96, 98
organizational structures 67–9, 85, 151–2

parameter design stage in Taguchi approach in design of experiments (technique) 126
Pareto voting 116, 122, 153
partnerships 1–8, 9–19, 91–100, 149–62
at Cosalt Holiday Homes 75–88
at Rover Group 39–57
at Tallent Engineering 59–74
barriers to 4–7
benefits 91–100, 101, 102, 107, 118–42
concept of 13–16
defined 60, 92
difficulties 158–9
drawbacks 95, 102
future prospects 101–9
in the public sector 21–36
long-term 2–4
monitoring of performance 142–5, 162
tools, techniques and systems 111–45
with small and medium size enterprises 78–81, 83
see also suppliers
payment terms 80
performance measurement 56, 64–7, 70, 108, 117, 142, 144
see also assessment of suppliers; benchmarking

planning 2–3, 42, 44, 53
power 7, 17, 18
    abuse 6, 18, 19
    imbalances 10
prices and pricing 5, 6, 31, 85, 87, 93, 103,
    161
    at Rover Group 40, 45
    reductions 22, 27
pro-active purchasing *see* partnerships
proactive measures of customer satisfac-
    tion 4–5
probity 21
problem solving 2, 3, 76, 119, 157, 159, 162
process cause and effect diagrams 121
process cost model 117
process management 3, 41, 55, 117,
    123–6, 136
procurement 22–4, 34–5, 67, 95, 152, 153–4
    at Rover Group 39–57
    by public bodies 22–7, 33–4
    economic objectives 33–4
    of services 27–30
    social policy objectives 33–4
product development *see* design of
    products; new product introduc-
    tion process; research and
    development
product liability 67
productivity 3, 22, 60, 67, 76
profit and profitability 45–6, 63, 87, 93,
    101
project management 40, 45, 57, 114, 136,
    158
Public Accounts Committee 25–6, 35
public sector partnerships 21–36
    legislation 24–5, 27–8, 35
purchased supplies
    at Rover Group 40, 56
    quality 1, 3
    see also procurement
purchasing *see* procurement
purchasing power 6–7, 86
purchasing quality strategy (Rover
    Group) 42–6

QCDDM (Nissan supplier rating
    system) 144
quality control circles 75–7, 119
quality costing 112, 116–8

quality function deployment analysis
    133, 135–8, 160
quality management systems 7, 41, 42,
    47, 49, 51, 64, 68, 69, 71, 73, 75–7, 78,
    80–81, 83, 86, 87, 88, 93, 94, 111, 117,
    126, 139–42, 155–6, 161
    documentation 139
    standards (British and international)
        8, 41, 76–7, 139–42
    see also failure mode and effects
        analysis
quality of supplies/services 1, 3, 22, 29,
    32, 47, 67–8
    planning 5
quality operating system (at Ford) 64
quotation analysis forms 45

Rank Xerox (company) 112–3
reactive measures of customer satisfac-
    tion 4–5
relationships *see* partnerships
reliability 158
    analysis of 5, 127
reputation 3
research and development 24, 54, 136,
    150
    see also design of products; new
        product introduction process
respect 85
responsibilities 2, 67, 68, 69
RG 2000 business model 41, 49, 53, 99
risk and revenue sharing partnerships
    13
risk priority number (in FMEA) 129–30
risks 30
rogue suppliers 80, 81, 85, 86
Rover Employee Assisted Learning 56
Rover Group 39–57, 65
Rover Learning Business 55
Rover Tomorrow (strategy) 47, 48

sanctions 17, 19
schedules 6
    changing 5
security of supplies 3
segmentation of customer/supplier base
    108
self-interest 2
social services procurement 30–2

Somerfield stores (company) 104, 105
sourcing 69, 71, 72, 98–9, 105, 152, 154–5
   at Cosalt Holiday Homes 77
   at Rover Group 39, 51
   see also suppliers
stability of supplies 3
standards (British and international) 8, 41, 76–7, 139–42
statistical process control 64, 142, 156, 160
strategic needs 107
strategic sourcing 154
strategy core groups 44
suggestions for improvement 87, 119, 159
   see also ideas
supplier development teams
   at Nissan 64, 105
   at Rover Group 56, 65
supplier partnerships *see* partnerships
supplier quality assurance 6, 69
supplier quality improvement 69
suppliers 1, 2, 39–57, 59–74, 64, 65, 78–81, 101–2, 105, 118, 149–50
   assessment of 41, 49, 53, 80–81, 96, 99, 155–8, 160
   development of 1, 44, 52, 56, 64–5, 77–8, 80, 91, 98, 105, 106, 150, 153
   in the public sector 21–36
   rating systems 144
   responsiveness 3
   role in design and R&D 3, 40–41, 47, 60, 154
   see also partnerships
supply chains 5, 9, 16, 17, 44, 46, 47, 48, 50, 51, 55, 57, 60, 62, 66, 68, 69–70, 149, 157–8
   improvement of 108–9
   management 10
survival-of-the-fittest approach to partnership 105–6
SWOT analyses 81
synergy 115
system design stage in Taguchi approach in design of experiments (technique) 124
systems for developing partnerships 111–45

T-type matrix diagrams 133

Taguchi approach in design of experiments (technique) 124–6
Tallent Engineering 59–74
TBP *see* total business performance
teamworking 42, 68, 69, 121–2, 129, 136, 152
techniques for developing partnerships 111–45
tendering 7, 21–36
threats 19
Thyssen Group 59
tolerance design stage in Taguchi approach in design of experiments (technique) 126
tooling 4, 6, 47, 49, 55
tools for developing partnerships 111–45
total business performance 41
total quality improvement 41
total quality management 6, 9, 42
   of people 49
TQI *see* total quality improvement
TQM *see* total quality management
trail and error method in design of experiments (technique) 123
training 24, 44, 53, 55–6, 68, 96, 98, 123
transaction costs 29, 32, 104, 106
trust 2, 17, 18, 19, 32, 52, 60, 63, 85, 94, 96, 99, 104, 105, 160
TX96 (Tallent excellence target) 66, 70

understanding 70
   lack of 159

value chain management 49
value for money 3, 24, 26–7, 29, 36, 66
values 57, 80, 96, 112, 145, 160, 162
vendor assessment system 70
vendor managed inventory (technique) 104
Volkswagen (company) 82
voting 116

waste 46, 47, 118
White Paper on Goverrnment Procurement Strategy (1995) 23, 30
win-win negotiations 24, 85, 93

Y-type matrix diagrams 133

Gower Handbook of Customer Service

Edited by Peter Murley

In a world dominated by look-alike products at similar prices, superior customer service may be the only available route to competitive advantage. This Gower Handbook brings together no fewer than 32 professionals in the field, each one a recognized expert on his or her subject. Using examples and case studies from a variety of businesses, they examine the entire range of customer service activities, from policy formulation to telephone technique.

The material is presented in six parts:

- Customer Service in Context
- Measuring, Modelling, Planning
- Marketing Customer Service
- The Cultural Dimension
- The Human Ingredient
- Making the Most of Technology

For anyone concerned with customer satisfaction, whether in the private or the public sector, the Handbook is an unrivalled source of information, ideas and practical guidance.

Gower

Gower Handbook of Management Skills

Third Edition

Edited by Dorothy M Stewart

'This is the book I wish I'd had in my desk drawer when I was first a manager. When you need the information, you'll find a chapter to help; no fancy models or useless theories. This is a practical book for real managers, aimed at helping you manage more effectively in the real world of business today. You'll find enough background information, but no overwhelming detail. This is material you can trust. It is tried and tested.'

So writes Dorothy Stewart, describing in the preface the unifying theme behind the new edition of this bestselling Handbook. This puts at your disposal the expertise of 25 specialists, each a recognized authority in their particular field. Together, this adds up to an impressive 'one stop library' for the manager determined to make a mark.

Chapters are organised within three parts: Managing Yourself, Managing Other People, and Managing Business. Part I deals with personal skills and includes chapters on self-development and information technology. Part II covers people skills such as listening, influencing and communication. Part III looks at finance, project management, decision-making, negotiating and creativity. A total of 12 chapters are completely new, and the rest have been rigorously updated to fully reflect the rapidly changing world in which we work.

Each chapter focuses on detailed practical guidance, and ends with a checklist of key points and suggestions for further reading.

Gower

Managing Customer Service

Jenny Hayes and Frances Dredge

Excellent customer service is now considered as an indispensable part of any successful company. Yet what this means for the customer service manager or supervisor, in practical terms, is often overlooked. *Managing Customer Service* is written for them.

It provides a concise introduction to the business reasons for building good relationships with customers, examines the management framework of customer service, explains the customer service manager's role, and then offers techniques that are easy to implement for improved customer service.

Very much a 'hands-on' guide, *Managing Customer Service* deals with all the real and demanding issues that a manager or supervisor has to face on a day to day basis. Topics include:

• communication methods: from telephone skills to the challenge of the Internet
• dealing with difficult and angry customers
• turning opportunities into new sales.

Gower

Managing Relationship Selling

David W Smith

Relationship selling is distinct from all other approaches to selling. It is the only approach proven to give consistently excellent results, where 'high-ticket' selling is combined with a selling 'relationship'.

David Smith's manual is designed to enable both the sales manager and the salesperson to make relationship selling a success in their organization. It is divided into three sections:

Part 1 explores how you, as Sales Manager, should add value to your salespeople at every stage of the sales cycle. This section explains the differences between relationship selling and other forms, and the role of the Sales Manager in managing the process.

Part 2 deals with specific skills of relationship selling. It broadly follows the progress of the sale from beginning to end and provides concise techniques, examples, checklists and exercises covering all of the key skills needed.

Part 3 presents three tools for effective sales coaching: the Learning Log, the Sales Objective and the Sales Coaching Guide. It also includes 12 exercises for you to develop understanding of both the relationship selling process and the requisite skills in your sales team.

The mixture of down-to-earth techniques and ideas for the sales manager and exercises for developing skills, make this manual an extremely practical tool for all sales managers and anyone involved in developing relationship selling skills.

Gower